DISRUPTING THE ACADEMY WITH LIVED EXPERIENCE-LED KNOWLEDGE

Key Issues in Social Justice: Voices from the Frontline

Series Editors: **Kalwant Bhopal**, University of Birmingham, **Martin Myers**, University of Nottingham, **Karl Kitching**, University of Birmingham and **Kenzo Sung**, Rowan Univeristy

How do issues of social justice, inclusion and equity shape modern day society? This series delivers a forum for perspectives from historically marginalised and minoritised communities to challenge contemporary dominant discourses about social justice, inclusion and equity in the social sciences and aligned disciplines.

Also available

Permanent Racism:
Race, Class and the Myth of Post-racial Britain
By **Paul Warmington**

Low-income Female Teacher Values and Agency in India:
Implications for Reflective Practice
By **Ruth Samuel**

Transformative Teaching and Learning in Further Education:
Pedagogies of Hope and Social Justice
By **Rob Smith and Vicky Duckworth**

Hidden Voices:
Lived Experiences in the Irish Welfare Space
By **Joe Whelan**

Find out more

policy.bristoluniversitypress.co.uk/
key-issues-in-social-justice

DISRUPTING THE ACADEMY WITH LIVED EXPERIENCE-LED KNOWLEDGE

Edited by
Maree Higgins and Caroline Lenette

P

First published in Great Britain in 2024 by

Policy Press, an imprint of
Bristol University Press
University of Bristol
1–9 Old Park Hill
Bristol
BS2 8BB
UK
t: +44 (0)117 374 6645
e: bup-info@bristol.ac.uk

Details of international sales and distribution partners are available at policy.bristoluniversitypress.co.uk

British Library Cataloguing in Publication Data
A catalogue record for this book is available from the British Library

ISBN 978-1-4473-6633-1 hardcover
ISBN 978-1-4473-6634-8 paperback
ISBN 978-1-4473-6635-5 ePub
ISBN 978-1-4473-6636-2 ePdf

Cover design: Liam Roberts Design
Front cover image: unsplash/FLY:D

The book contains some disturbing content, such as mentions of sexual abuse, self-harm and discussion of suicidal thoughts/ideation.

Maree:
For Jasmine, my guiding star, for Jon, keeper of my heart.
And for all whose wisdom and experiences are shared in this book.

Caroline:
For the women who came before me, whose lived experiences remain
partially unknown. Lise Gabrielle Béchard Lenette (1914–1971), her
mother Marie Lucia Justine Béchard and her grandmother Lucie
Courtois Maclou. Denise Jean-Louis Ménélas (b. 1935), her mother
Marie Suzanne Jean-Louis Phanjoo (1918–2012) and her grandmother
Louise Sylvia Yvonne Souci.
And for Lucie. I enjoy watching you grow up.

Contents

Series editor's preface

Kalwant Bhopal (University of Birmingham)

Debates about social justice, inclusion and equity in the early 21st century have become increasingly more contentious and problematical. This should not come as a surprise and reflects western social, economic and political climates driven by neoliberal narratives; the rapid expansion of European Union membership followed by signs of its impending potential dissolution; the election of Donald Trump as 45th president of the United States in 2016; and the growing populism of nationalist political parties in almost every western democracy. At the same time the global south has seen economic expansion on a scale undreamt of a generation ago that threatens to undermine the hegemony of the west.

This original book series delivers a forum for marginalised and minoritised perspectives in the social sciences. It challenges contemporary dominant discourses about social justice, inclusion and equity from the perspective of marginalised and minoritised communities. Drawing upon the work of researchers, theorists and practitioners from Europe, the United States and the global south, the series adopts a broad interdisciplinary approach including disciplines such as education, sociology, social policy and childhood studies. The titles in the series are published on broad topics, underpinned by research and theory.

The series draws upon definitions of social justice that identify the marginalisation and exclusion of groups and communities of people based on their difference from the majority population. The series seeks to understand how such processes should be disrupted and subverted. Social justice in this respect is both the subject matter of the book series but also its practical contribution to academic scholarship. By providing an outlet for scholarship that itself emerges from under-represented voices the books published in the series contribute to addressing rather than simply commenting on social justice issues. The series centre social justice, inclusion and equity as a key focus; gives voice to those from marginalised communities and groups; places a spotlight on the work of under-represented (minority ethnic, religious, disabled, female, LGBTQIA+) academics; and challenges hegemonic narratives that underpin western discourses about how best to reach a socially just world.

A key strength of the series includes a broad range of topics from different disciplines in the social sciences including education, sociology, social policy, gender studies, migration and international relations, politics and childhood studies. The series draws on themes which include race/ethnicity, gender, class, sexuality, age, poverty, disability and other topics which address and challenge inequalities. It includes a range of different theoretical perspectives including addressing intersectional identities.

This important edited collection focuses on examples of lived experience scholarship that is both emancipatory and decolonial – one that is much needed in present times. It examines how agency and knowledge of marginalised groups is key in understanding the workings of experience-led knowledge. The diverse range of contributions examine the importance of intersectional experiences, particularly in relation to exploring collaborative research and methodologies. This edited collection provides an original contribution to examining how lived experience can be used to disrupt and decolonise academic research, with a key focus on how practices can be used to transform social justice in the academy.

List of figures

Notes on contributors

Seini Afeaki is from the Kingdom of Tonga. She is a fearless advocate with a purpose for Pacific communities in New South Wales (NSW), Australia, for the last 30-plus years. She has worked across government and non-government agencies in different capacities and currently with the NSW Children's Court Clinic. Her postgraduate training is on project management and policy development. She has served on different boards including the NSW Community Relations Commission as a commissioner and is currently Senior Advisor to the Pacific Women's Professional Business Network and Chairperson of the Pacific Mental Health Initiative.

Maherau Arona was born in Dunedin, Aotearoa New Zealand. Her father is from Rakahanga, and her mother is from Penryhn, Cook Islands. She resides in Sydney, Australia and works for Mission Australia as Youth Justice Conference Convenor. She is President of the Pacific Islands Mount Druitt Action Network Inc and Team Manager for the Cook Islands Rugby League Women's World Cup Team. She studied at Otago University, and previously worked at Child Youth and Families New Zealand.

Atem Dau Atem has recently finished a PhD exploring the settlement experience of South Sudanese humanitarian migrants in Western Sydney. Atem was born in South Sudan. He came to Australia as a refugee. He is President of NSW Refugee Communities Advocacy Network. He works for the NSW Service for the Treatment and Rehabilitation of Torture and Trauma Survivors.

Campbell Clerke is a member of the Lived Experience team that worked with the Black Dog Institute in Australia.

William Crompton is a 27-year-old man working as an electrician travelling around Australia, constructing and maintaining airports. This work takes him away from home for a significant part of the year and often to remote parts of the country and has led William to experience some very dark times, exacerbated by isolation, alcohol abuse and relationship difficulties. Taking his own life has never seemed too far away. Since advocating for improved mental health and challenging himself through athletic achievements, William's situation has improved significantly. He is a member of the Lived Experience team that worked with the Black Dog Institute.

Deb Evans is a Malyangapa/Ngiyampaa *wiimpatja* from Far Western New South Wales who loves returning home regularly. Deb has lived and worked on Wiradyuri Country since 1994 and is thankful for her deep connections with Wongamaa, Pastor Cec Grant (deceased), Uncle Stan Grant (Senior) and several other key Wiradyuri Elders, many of whom still guide her given she is living and working on someone else's Country. Deb is passionate about renewing language, and Indigenous nation rebuilding as a way of recovering Indigenous cultural lifeways in order to live according to Indigenous worldviews.

Malaemie Fruean is Chair of the New South Wales Council for Pacific Communities. Both her mother and father are from Ngapuhi associated with the Northland region of Aotearoa New Zealand and centred in the Hokianga, the Bay of Islands and Whangārei. She has worked within the community for several years at TAFE NSW (technical college), Mission Australia, Campbelltown City Council and One Door Mental Health. She currently manages the South West Multicultural and Community Centre and South West Multicultural and Community Centre. She has a BA in adult education from the University of Technology Sydney. She was awarded the Order of Australia Medal in 2022.

Uncle Stan Grant (Senior) is a Wiradyuri Elder who received national recognition from his own people when he won the prestigious National Aboriginal and Islander Day Observance Committee Lifetime Achievement Award in 2022 for his tireless work to renew the ancestral language of his people. Along with his non-Indigenous brother, Dr John Rudder, Uncle Stan has undertaken remarkable work in reclaiming the Wiradyuri language, which has led to the development of a multiple award-winning Graduate Certificate of Wiradjuri Language, Culture and Heritage at Charles Sturt University under the direction of Wiradyuri Elders and other nation builders.

Sue Green is Professor of Indigenous Studies at Charles Sturt University. Sue completed a social work degree and went on to study a PhD in which she asked questions about how do we decolonise, and how does she decolonise? A few years ago, Sue was asked to come home to take up the role of Course Director for the Wiradyuri language course at Charles Sturt University. Along with her husband, children and grandchildren, Sue moved back to Country. Sue shifted from teaching social work to teaching within the Wiradyuri language course. Sue works alongside Wiradyuri people and Wiradyuri allies who are walking the journey of Wiradyuri language restoration and the rebuilding of the Wiradyuri nation.

Yassin Ali Hadu has been working as Chairman of Gerakan untuk Kesejahteraan Tuna Rungu Indonesia (Gerkatin, Movement for Indonesian Deaf Peoples Welfare) in Central Sulawesi Province since 2009. After surviving the earthquake, tsunami and liquefaction that hit Central Sulawesi in 2018, he participated in providing humanitarian assistance with other organisations of people with disabilities. Since then, he has been working with different non-governmental organisations and partnering with Arbeiter-Samariter-Bund Indonesia and the Philippines in various programmes related to disability inclusion in water, sanitation and hygiene, safe schools, disaster risk reduction, COVID-19 response, localisation of humanitarian actions, and accessibility assessment. He is actively advocating for the empowerment and equality of people with disabilities, especially Deaf people, in numerous initiatives.

Letitia Harris was taught her language as an adult by her Elders. She has grown in Wiradyuri language teaching, learning to teach beside her Elders and being instructed by them. She continues to work under the instruction of her Elders to revitalise Wiradyuri language for their nation. *Yiradhu marang, bala-dhu guyal dharran-giyalang. Ngadhu yali-nyal badhiin-gu-bu babiin-gu-bu ngiyang. Yuwin-dhu Yaladidya. Bala-dhu Wiradyuri!* (Good day, I belong to Cooyal Creek. I speak to you in the language of my grandmother and father. My name is Letetia. I am Wiradyuri!).

Maree Higgins is Senior Lecturer in the School of Social Sciences and Social Work Lead in the Big Anxiety Research Centre at the University of New South Wales. She is a leading social work scholar with experience in international social work, asylum seeker advocacy and youth work. Maree researches lived experience through a distinctive combination of trauma-informed, strength-based and critical methodologies. She is dedicated to transforming thinking and practice in human rights through creative collaboration and cultural innovation and focuses on contemporary social justice issues experienced by people from refugee backgrounds, older people, people with serious mental illness and missing girls.

Elias Katapi is working as Chairman of Persatuan Tuna Netra Indonesia (Pertuni, Indonesian Blind Association) in Central Sulawesi Province. He is also currently working as a masseur and managing church development in his community. He has been actively advocating for the rights of people with disabilities, especially in accessibility, inclusion, education and employment. Since surviving the 2018 Central Sulawesi disasters, he has been collaborating with different non-governmental organisations in various projects on humanitarian assistance, disaster preparedness training, research on inclusive water, sanitation, and hygiene, and community economic empowerment. He has significant experience facilitating capacity-building activities for disaster risk reduction at the village level, especially in Sigi and Donggala districts.

Chrysant Lily Kusumowardoyo works as Country Director of Arbeiter-Samariter-Bund Indonesia and the Philippines. Since joining this organisation in 2016, she has been working with organisations of people with disabilities and continues to learn new ways to establish eye-level partnerships, particularly in disability-inclusive disaster risk reduction and humanitarian response. She lives in Yogyakarta, Indonesia, with her husband, a dog, a cat and many house plants.

Stephen Lake completed a double honours in Theology and History at Flinders University, and a PhD in Medieval History at Cambridge University. He held research and teaching positions at the Sorbonne, Bamberg and Constance in Medieval Philosophy, Medieval History and Classics. He is currently completing a second PhD in 20th-century German Philosophy at the University of Sydney. His engagement with the Black Dog Institute enables him to combine lived experience and scholarly expertise in advocating for whole-of-society social justice responses to mental health and suicide that promotes meaning and purpose in the lives of people living with complex trauma and its effects.

Harry Lambshead's language journey commenced when he was a baby through his mother speaking Wiradyuri words to him. However, as he grew older, he moved away from practising his culture until a workplace injury, which gave him the opportunity to re-evaluate his life. *Baladhu Wiradyuri-giyalang gurawalar-i gunhinarrung-gu ngurambang. Yuwin-dhu Yarri* (I be Wiradyuri belonging from Koorawatha, my grandmother's country. My name is Harry). My grandmother Edna May Gilbert and my mother Gloria Lambshead are the mothers who placed me and told me I am Wiradyuri.

Caroline Lenette is Associate Professor, School of Social Sciences and Deputy Director of the Big Anxiety Research Centre at the University of New South Wales. She is a leading interdisciplinary researcher focusing on participatory methods, social justice informed research especially with refugee-background co-researchers, and how we conceptualise ethics in participatory research practice. Her work focuses on decolonising research methods by revaluing Indigenous and majority-world knowledges. Caroline is the author of *Arts-Based Methods in Refugee Research: Creating Sanctuary* (2019, Springer) and *Participatory Action Research: Ethics and Decolonization* (2022, Oxford University Press).

Ivan Ma is a member of the Lived Experience team that worked with the Black Dog Institute in Australia.

Rebecca J. Moran has a practice background in youth work, domestic violence services, mental health, training and criminology research. She has specialised in complex trauma and recovery for many years and has served as a trainer and consultant for government and non-government agencies in Australia and the United Kingdom for over a decade. Rebecca is Lived Experience Engagement Fellow in the Big Anxiety Research Centre at the University of New South Wales and is completing her PhD in the School of Social Sciences. Rebecca also has lived experience of trauma and recovery and draws on a mix of professional and personal experience in her work.

Donna Murray is Wiradyuri with kinship connections to the people of the (Murrumbidga) Murrumbidgee and (Galari) Lachlan rivers. Growing up on Country provided Donna the opportunity to know, spend time, listen and learn from her old people and extended family, although as a young person, hearing her grandfather's and father's yarns, she didn't really understand the significance of storytelling.

John O'Loughlin has wondered for some time now if there was any mental health help available to him as someone on a low income, who could not afford long-term professional help. In the face of daily struggles, he was often left to find a solution himself. Becoming a Lived Experience Adviser with the Black Dog Institute has given John the resources and network to manage his mental health more effectively.

Estelle Keerthana (legal name Hari Hara Sudhan) Ramaswamy is a Thirunangai (a Tamil equivalent to transwoman). She is Australia's first international trans and gender non-binary (Thirunangai) PhD student from Chennai, India. Estelle Keerthana is a fierce activist for LGBTQIA+ human rights and is a strong First Nations ally channelling her activism through Ardham Collective and Social Trust in Australia and India. She is currently working on a Tamil Nadu State government project implementing Sustainable Development Goals in Kanyakumari district. She is a member of the Gender Equality Taskforce for the City of Casey, Victoria, Australia.

Jioji Ravulo is Professor and Chair of Social Work and Policy Studies at the University of Sydney. His father is iTaukei (Indigenous) Fijian, and his late mother is Anglo Australian. He has lived and worked most of his personal and professional life in various areas of Greater Western Sydney. His academic life has included working with the University of the South Pacific, providing opportunities to collaborate across the Pacific region and beyond.

Irmansyah Songgoua is working as the secretary of the local branch of Perkumpulan Penyandang Disabilitas Indonesia (Indonesian Association of People with Disabilities) in Palu, Central Sulawesi. As a survivor of the disasters that hit Central Sulawesi in 2018, he has collaborated with international and local non-government organisations for inclusive disaster risk reduction initiatives in Central Sulawesi. His experiences include facilitating capacity building activities, actively participating in disaster evacuation simulations at the village level, contributing to the improvement of public services accessibility for people with disabilities, and co-researching for inclusive water, sanitation and hygiene research. He believes people with disabilities must be the subject, not the object, of humanitarian actions, and he has been working to realise this.

Norman Stevens is a 70-year-old retired sales manager who unfortunately retired early because of mental health problems. Norman grew up in Brisbane, Australia, as one of five children (two boys and three girls). His father was a police officer and strict disciplinarian. Norman's childhood was traumatic, and he was subjected to physical and verbal abuse until the age of 16 when he left home. At 19, Norman moved to Perth which is now his home. The trauma of his childhood was to revisit Norman in his early 50s, and he attempted to end his life. That in turn led to being a member of the Lived Experience team that worked with the Black Dog Institute and the University of New South Wales in the creation of this book chapter.

Peter Sutton is a member of the Lived Experience team that worked with the Black Dog Institute in Australia.

Donina Va'a is Early Childhood Development Specialist Consultant with UNICEF Pacific, providing technical support to the Pacific Regional Council for Early Childhood Development, and Chair of the Pacific Women's Professional Business Network. Her father hails from Saoluafata, Upolu and mother from Sala'ilua, Savai'i. Born in Grey Lynn, Aotearoa New Zealand, she grew up in Samoa and Fiji; however, most of her professional life is in Sydney. She has also worked in Samoa, Fiji and Aotearoa New Zealand.

Matt Whitten is a member of the Lived Experience team that worked with the Black Dog Institute in Australia.

Husna Yuni Wulansari is working as Communication and Knowledge Management Coordinator of Arbeiter-Samariter-Bund Indonesia and the Philippines and the Disability-Inclusive Disaster Risk Reduction Network. Her previous research experiences at Arbeiter-Samariter-Bund Indonesia and Gadjah Mada University in Yogyakarta, Indonesia, sparked her interest to learn more about social inclusion and participation of the most at-risk groups in the fields of development and humanitarian aid.

Zainab works as the member of the local branch of Himpunan Wanita Disabilitas Indonesia (Indonesian Women with Disabilities Association) in Palu, Central Sulawesi. She has been managing her small business and actively participating in various non-governmental organisation-led disaster risk reduction projects in Palu. She survived the Central Sulawesi disasters in 2018, and, since then, she has worked with different humanitarian organisations for conducting post-disaster assessments, humanitarian response, capacity building and inclusive research. She is also involved in the local population census activities and working with the community-based integrated health-care centre in her district.

Acknowledgements

We pay our respects to the Traditional Custodians of the lands, winds and waters where we live, work and play, the Bedegal People of the Eora Nation. We are guests on this land. We acknowledge that we can write this book because of our privileges and the benefits that accrue to us because of the colonisation and dispossession of Aboriginal and Torres Strait Islander people. We are part of an academic institution built on Indigenous land. Sovereignty was never ceded. There was no consent, no treaty and no compensation. We acknowledge the violent history of this country, a violence that continues to this day in so-called Australia.

We are deeply honoured to have worked with this diverse group of chapter authors, who trusted us with their stories and perspectives. Each contributor, named as well as anonymous, shared their perspectives with generosity and integrity. Thank you for sitting with us in friendly (and unfriendly) cafés, in offices and on garden benches, and in Zoom meetings to think about how you could disrupt the academy. We are very grateful for the privilege of working with you to develop and share these insights. We acknowledge and thank you for all your time and effort – this book would not exist without you!

Note on the figures

The figures in Chapter 4 have been published in greyscale, as per our house style. For colour versions of these figures, please visit https://bristoluniversitypress.co.uk/disrupting-the-academy-with-lived-experience-led-knowledge or the artist's website, www.campbellclerke.com.

Preface

In 2020, during an early morning walk at Centennial Park on Gadigal land in Eora Country, we floated the idea of writing a book about the marginal place of lived experience-led knowledge in the academy. The thought stemmed from our reflections on a co-designed project with refugee-background co-researchers on ethical practice principles in community-based participatory research, with team members in so-called Australia and England. We had the privilege of learning enormously through enriching knowledge sharing during our project discussions. But it left us wondering why this felt like such a rare occurrence despite our commitment to collaborative and participatory research.

While we proceeded on our walk, we discussed several frustrations linked to the realm of participatory research claiming to focus on lived experiences – including our own earlier research and publications, which were not immune to these shortcomings. We were complicit in a system we found faults with but did not challenge often enough.

We grappled with the commonplace academic writing practice of selecting decontextualised 'snippets' of people's narratives and use them as quotes to illustrate themes and arguments in publications claiming to convey lived experiences. We hardly question this norm. 'Lived experience' still has a largely *utilitarian* value instead of being considered a rich form of knowledge and expertise.

Another issue was the familiar experience of searching for scholarship on lived experiences of complex and multifaceted social justice issues, only to realise that authors are rarely people with relevant lived experiences. We were growing tired of this imposition of an outsider gaze and continual reliance on so-called expertise from western academic institutions and usually white, cisgender male, middle-aged, middle-class, ableist, Christian, English-speaking and heteronormative standpoints in knowledge production.

In our own research in refugee studies, we had shifted to co-research, co-production and co-authorship models to better reflect the contributions of people with lived experiences of forced migration – which we have not experienced personally – to the academy. But we had to admit that there were still problematic aspects.

First, we had readily accepted terms such as 'co-researchers' without questioning their meaning or impact on people with lived experiences. Our collaborator Jasmina Bajraktarevic-Hayward drew our attention to our uncritical use of this word and the assumption that a change from 'participant' to 'co-researcher' would resolve rather than *mask* power imbalances in research and knowledge co-production.

Second, due to our lack of attention to authorship, we had been passive consumers of social justice scholarship that produced skewed versions of lived realities and was elitist, white and western-based – hence our complicity in maintaining this norm. Third, our efforts to promote participatory models, co-produced research and co-authorship were far from enough to create a significant shift that could *disrupt* the academy.

We were on a steep learning curve. We have a combined 30 years of experience as researchers and we have only just begun to acknowledge our complicity in maintaining the status quo based on colonial practices, and our lack of attention to the implications of not doing enough to change it. We realised we had missed many opportunities to reflect in more depth on our own approaches – and we suspected that these issues were not unique to refugee studies.

We decided that, if we wanted to challenge and extend the scholarship on social justice issues in a meaningful way, our efforts had to focus squarely on lived experiences. This commitment is not just about 'inclusion' – a term we reject because of its banality, especially in institutional contexts. We aimed to explore how the academy uses and misuses, amplifies and misappropriates, respects and disregards knowledge grounded in the rich and textured day-to-day realities of people most affected by social injustices. Our deliberate focus on lived experience aims to cede space in the academy for those who hold first-hand knowledge on the very issues others have claimed expertise on.

We decided to write the book we wish we had found in our initial scan of the literature for insightful examples of lived experience-led scholarship that is emancipatory and decolonial, and that values the agency and knowledge of people who experience injustices every day. Our shift to (re)centring lived experience-led knowledge as opposed to simply opting for a 'co-research' model (and hoping it would automatically resolve inherent power imbalances and colonial structures) problematises tokenistic takes on collaborative research, of which there are far too many examples in the academy.

Clearly, we could not be the sole authors due to our positionalities and privileges, as that would go against the very problem we sought to address. Our choice of key social justice issues for an edited book was based on our knowledge of disciplines where the literature on co-research, co-production and participatory research is growing but does not sufficiently privilege lived experience-led perspectives. We considered our networks of colleagues – and developed new ones – across disciplines to provide intersectional explorations that can enrich our knowledge of collaborative research and methodologies.

This project has not been without challenges. The omnipresent threat of the COVID-19 pandemic and the changing landscape of our work environment made each step towards producing this edited collection more arduous. We tried to maintain the principles of collegiality and flexibility throughout the process, especially because of the writing model we chose to privilege (see Chapter 1).

And the outcome did not disappoint. From the time we approached potential contributors to discuss the idea, we were both heartened by their immediate and positive responses. One such reply read: 'Not a lot of spaces to publish work like this and I am grateful for it.' This reaction confirmed our initial impression that lived experience-led knowledge was intentionally kept at the margins, and this needs to change.

For this book to come together, we could not maintain a 'distant' role as editors. It was not simply a matter of sharing a call for chapters with deadlines to meet. We had to think carefully about potential authors and develop new and meaningful relationships, and discuss ideas and uncertainties, the problems they encountered, and issues they grappled with. This approach was hard work, and we have learned a lot from contributors about writing focused on lived experiences. We experienced how respectful engagement in the process of developing and sharing narratives can lead to transformative outcomes.

We still have much to (un)learn. We are part of institutions that reinforce rather than disrupt established approaches. Despite our commitment to reflexivity and decolonisation, we often miss opportunities to examine our own limitations and complicity. Even though we started this project from a place of humility and our motivation to disrupt norms in the academy and in social justice research, we were also deeply challenged on issues we thought we had a good grasp of.

We are proud of what this book will add to debates on social justice research. We hope that its contents will stimulate engaging and insightful discussions and extend reflections on how we can all conduct research differently.

Unpacking disruptive methodologies: what do we know about lived experience-led knowledge and scholarship?

Maree Higgins and Caroline Lenette

Key points

- Lived experience-led knowledge and scholarship have disruptive and decolonial potentials that have not been recognised to their just value in the academy.
- Revaluing knowledge grounded in first-hand experiences can contribute to redressing ongoing epistemic injustices in research and the body of knowledge on social justice.
- To expand current debates on lived experience, culturally safe and community-led methodologies can challenge outsider-imposed views.
- In line with the decolonial aims of this book, disruptive methodologies of knowledge production, namely Indigenous nation building, *talanoa*, autoethnography and collaborative autoethnography, are used to explore and share lived experience-led knowledge.
- Lived experience-led expertise is a rich form of knowledge that disrupts and decolonises long-held notions about whose knowledge counts in academia and why.

Introduction

The aim of this book is to disrupt and decolonise academic research using a lived experience lens. It prioritises the perspectives of people with first-hand experiences of key social justice issues, who use diverse methodologies to share their knowledge and expertise. Collectively, the authors challenge readers and researchers to *rethink* how they value knowledge grounded in lived experiences and how they should engage with lived experience-led research and scholarship. The authors' perspectives and critiques enrich current debates on how lived experience is used in research with a social justice concern. Their contributions prompt crucial reflections on the impacts of centring lived experience-led knowledge in research. The unique insights and practices that inform this book aim to transform social justice research and enrich multiple disciplines in the academy.

We first outline contextual definitions of lived experience and the complexities of using this lens. We state the decolonial intent of prioritising lived experience-led knowledge as a central concern of this book. We then describe the relevance of lived experience-led scholarship (including community-oriented models) to social justice research. We define four disruptive methodologies of knowledge production used in this book: Indigenous nation building, *talanoa*, autoethnography and collaborative autoethnography. After explaining the writing process, book structure and chapter-by-chapter summaries, we conclude by stating our positionalities.

Contextual notions of lived experience

Lived experience is an important site of knowledge and is framed as one of many forms of expertise or knowing. In academia, lived experience is usually situated as part of reflective research practices (Barnacle, 2004) based on the premise that people with first-hand experiences know the nuances and complexities of their experiences and are best placed to speak about them. While definitions vary across contexts, Moran and colleagues (2022: 2) define lived experience as 'a representation of our human experiences', so that in academia, '[t]he contribution of people with lived experience is a form of testimonio, rejecting ideas of singular "truths" and tidy narratives' (Moran et al, 2022: 5). In mental health research, for instance, the term 'people with lived experience' is used as a 'catch-phrase to designate those who speak directly to "living" lives affected by mental illness' (Costa et al, 2012: 86).

Culturally specific notions offer contextual insights on lived experience. Vivian and colleagues (2017) explore research *by*, *for* and *with* Indigenous peoples and define lived experience as deeply connected to Indigenous self-determination and sovereignty. This model of lived experience is grounded in Aboriginal and Torres Strait Islander ethics and culture, and is political, relational, restorative and reflexive about power (Rigney et al, 2022: 4–6). The Indigenous Lived Experience Centre from a leading mental health and suicide prevention research organisation in Australia (Black Dog Institute, 2023) co-developed a definition in consultation with Aboriginal and Torres Strait Islander lived experience representatives. The definition recognises the impacts and ongoing harms of colonisation on the health and wellbeing of Aboriginal and Torres Strait Islander people and the significant difference in conceptualisations and experiences of mental health and suicide for Indigenous and non-Indigenous people.

Community-oriented understandings of lived experience are underpinned by communal values, morals and ethical principles and can foster collective meaning-making processes (Kamwaria and Katola, 2012), producing knowledge that is fundamental to community life and individual wellbeing. In the context of Pasifika research, Naufahu (2018) drew on their Tongan identity to develop the concept of *talaloto*, a personal testimony of one's lived experiences, as an alternative, meaningful and authentic approach to documenting and sharing Pasifika knowledge. *Talaloto* means to 'tell all, reveal or share honestly lived realities that are deep within your mind and heart at a particular time. Talaloto is about mo'oni (truth), to'a (bravery), totonu (honesty), fakamo'oni (testimony) and nothing else but the true lived experiences of a person' (Naufahu, 2018: 18).

For Kara (2022), 'all human experience is lived experience', and the term 'experts by experience' might better reflect the value of an approach based on first-hand accounts. This points to the importance of deconstructing who 'experts' are in research with a social justice concern. Alonso Bejarano and colleagues (2019: 6–7) criticise researchers who 'just interpret the lives of others, building their careers by fueling the academic machine', especially those employed at universities as 'the place of absolute privilege' from which they speak and write. Until recently, the unquestioned norm in academia was to impose an outsider, expert gaze to interpret the lived experiences of the 'other'. By 'other', we mean situating those who are outside the (white[1]) normative space as stereotypical, inferior or unknowable (Hage, 1999). But as Barnacle (2004: 59) pointed out, '[o]ne might wonder … how it is possible to engage in description and interpretation of phenomena without in some sense also moving away from an original "immediacy" of lived experience', meaning that discussing an experience with detachment (or from a non-lived experience perspective) cannot have the same impact as first-hand accounts. This critique highlights the problem of privileging academic, and oftentimes outsider, expertise over lived experience-led knowledge (see, for instance, Tuhiwai Smith, 2021), which is at the heart of what this book aims to address.

Drawing from Munanjahli and South Sea Islander scholar Chelsea Watego's critique of anthropology, a discipline built 'off the backs of Blacks' (2021: 139) while claims of expertise lie solely with those with power and (white) privilege, we argue that centring lived experience-led knowledge is an emancipatory research approach with disruptive and decolonial potentials that have not been recognised to their just value in the academy. By prioritising the views and expertise of people who experience social injustices every day, we privilege knowledge grounded in first-hand experiences from authors with limited opportunities to disrupt and decolonise the academy. Thus, we reject the 'narrative erasure' (Baldwin, 2013 in Johnstone, 2021: 638) that characterises many disciplines with tokenistic commitments to lived experience-led knowledge and social justice.

Barnacle (2004: 61) argues that lived experience is 'not just an alternative site of knowledge production, but, rather, a *privileged* site of knowledge production' (emphasis added). While some forms of lived experience-led knowledge such as personal written accounts, anecdotes, letters, film, poetry, artworks, dance and literature have gained some recognition in the academy (Holman Jones et al, 2016; Vivian et al, 2017), lived experience expertise is still considered as peripheral rather than as a legitimate form of knowledge in the academy.

Complexities of lived experience-led research

Centring lived experiences and exposing the power relations that suppress them in research require deep listening, continuous reflection, tenacity and moral courage. Such work strengthens and re-orients disciplines such as social work (Dorozenko et al, 2016; Penak and Allen, 2022), health (Johnstone, 2021; Watego et al, 2021), social welfare (Wright and Patrick, 2019; Ryan and El Ayadi, 2020), sociology (Mathers et al, 2018; Álvarez and Coolsaet, 2020) and anthropology (Ginsberg and Rapp, 2020; Mahmud, 2021). Lived experience-led research can yield important counter-narratives to prejudices and stereotypes and address the silencing and marginalisation of 'othered' perspectives (Johnstone, 2021). Sharing lived experiences in research can also constitute small acts of resistance within rigid and depersonalising structures such as the psychiatric system (Costa et al, 2012).

However, as Barnacle (2004: 66) states, we can appreciate the 'virtues' and 'the significance of lived experience and, at the same time, its problematical status'. Leading Indigenous and decolonial scholars such as Eve Tuck and Linda Tuhiwai Smith have critiqued how certain kinds of lived experiences are consistently over-researched, producing damage-focused narratives that rob people of knowledge and their rights to share stories on their own terms (Tuck, 2009; Tuhiwai Smith, 2021). Watego (2021: 140) argued that Indigenous people 'can testify but never theorise', which speaks to the utilitarian treatment of lived experience-led knowledge.

Referring to the psychiatric system, Costa and colleagues (2012: 85) highlighted the exploitative use of lived experience and personal stories to further the interests of mental health organisations, resulting in 'disability tourism' and 'patient porn'. Such organisations can 'absorb resistance accounts, sanitize them, and carry them forward in ways that are useful for them, without disrupting their dominant practices' (Costa et al, 2012: 87), while ignoring other narratives. Failure to provide respectful platforms to share lived experience can result in deep wounding and harm, and persistent experiences of epistemic exclusion can undermine a person's sense of humanity (Johnstone, 2021). Moran and colleagues (2022: 5) agree that 'the inclusion of "lived experience" or sharing of personal testimonies is subject to co-option and commodification', with a tendency to rely on experiential categories and diagnoses that erase intersectional oppression and marginalisation. This might lead to silencing narratives that 'don't fit'.

Not all lived experiences are translatable for contexts where rigid standards dictate what counts as knowledge. First, some experiences and ideas can only be conveyed in first, traditional or Indigenous languages, and conveying them in English (for instance) loses the essence of the message and aligns ideas with different values (see Sweeney's vignette in Tuhiwai Smith, 2021: xxii). Second, translating experiences can involve immense pain, and for some experiences, there are no words in any language. Third, not all experiences *have* to be revealed or translated for an audience. The pursuit of knowledge does not always mean articulating untranslatable experience for others' consumption – an academic norm linked to colonial imperatives (see Lenette, 2022). The notion of refusal as a political alternative to colonial society, as Kahnawà:ke Mohawk scholar Audra Simpson (2017) explains, can counter the power imbalances inherent to 'seeking' recognition within colonial structures – refusal is about Indigenous sovereignty.

Thus, Costa and colleagues (2012: 96) urged researchers 'to complicate what we are listening for' and favour 'more for stories of resistance and opposition, collective action and social change', since a selective use of sanitised narratives as the only form of lived experience-led knowledge does little to change the very structures that marginalise and reinforce social injustices. In some cases, this exploitative approach serves to further hurt and humiliate those who impart their knowledge based on lived experiences.

Decolonial aims

The editors and most of the contributors live and work in the country now called Australia, on sovereign, unceded and colonised Aboriginal and Torres Strait Islander land. The social, political, economic, spiritual, cultural, environmental and intellectual ramifications of colonisation (Wane, 2006), and the regional politics, trade and educational links with Asia and the Pacific, set the scene for the book's topics. The authorship reflects several socio-cultural and linguistic backgrounds, with contributors from the Wiradyuri Nation, one of over 250 First Nations language groups in Australia, and from colonised nations such as Aotearoa New Zealand, Indonesia, the Cook Islands and India. The harmful colonial values reproduced in western-centric research and knowledge production in this geographic region and the exploitative research processes imposed upon Indigenous communities and those with marginalised identities are well documented (see Vaioleti, 2013; Naufahu, 2018; Tuhiwai Smith, 2021; Watego, 2021; Lenette, 2022).

Many academic institutions continue to reflect the colonial values that justified their establishment (Moosavi, 2020) and uphold neoliberal, western–centric, and Eurocentric frameworks that maintain complicity with ongoing dispossession, marginalisation and oppression of Indigenous peoples and the 'other' (Alonso Bejarano et al, 2019; Penak and Allen, 2022). As such, academic research is rife with colonialist–infused methodologies that reinforce white, elitist and outsider-imposed ways of knowing (Moosavi, 2020; Lenette, 2022). This has resulted in perpetuating harmful approaches, especially in Indigenous research (Tuhiwai Smith, 2021; Watego, 2021). As Vivian and colleagues (2017: 50) point out, 'the colonised research orientation misidentifies what even counts as data'.

Decolonisation refers to 'repatriation of Indigenous land and life' (Tuck and Yang, 2012: 1) towards self-determination and sovereignty. As coloniality does not merely refer to historical events but is deeply entrenched and manifests daily in 'an entire structure of racialized and gendered power and social inequality', decolonisation refers to 'the process of undoing that inequality' (Alonso Bejarano et al, 2019: 20). It involves redressing the persistent harms of colonisation, including in knowledge production.

Decolonising the academy means ceding space for erased or marginalised knowledge systems and questioning researchers' positionalities and privileges to rectify the legacy of epistemicide – the killing of knowledge systems (Alonso Bejarano et al, 2019). Decolonising research explicitly rejects western–centric and colonial frameworks and amplifies research practices and knowledges that the academy has excluded, silenced, manipulated and 'epistemically demeaned as intellectually inferior and lacking credibility' (Johnstone, 2021: 637). As such, decolonising research is about epistemic justice in knowledge production. For Cook and colleagues (2019: 380), epistemic injustice 'forefronts the impact of prejudice, particularly the ongoing prejudice that leads to deflated levels of credibility for certain sectors of society'. Despite a growing interest in decolonial approaches and disruptive methodologies of knowledge production, the decolonisation agenda has progressed slowly (Tuhiwai Smith, 2021) due to our collective failure to challenge entrenched research norms.

In this book, the disruptive models of knowledge production emphasise how to 'understand and prioritize local conceptions of local realities, rather than just running those realities through the interpretive machinery of elite European social theory' (Alonso Bejarano et al, 2019: 8). A decolonial approach creates a publication space where 'people … may produce knowledge about themselves, for themselves' (Alonso Bejarano et al, 2019: 8).

Decolonising research also means upholding the values of cultural safety in knowledge production. This concept, grounded in Māori knowledge to disrupt racist attitudes in transcultural nursing in Aotearoa New Zealand, implies that 'there is *no assault on a person's identity*' (Williams, 1999: 213, original emphasis). Cultural safety in research – or culturally safe research – implies that it is participants who determine whether research practices and teams value and privilege their unique standpoints and perspectives (Lenette, 2022). When knowledge production processes are culturally safe, people can contribute their perspectives without fear of being judged, misunderstood or devalued, and their narratives are respected and recognised to their just value.

Lived experience-led knowledge and social justice research

Social justice is concerned with 'creating fair relations in terms of opportunity between people and society' (Cook et al, 2019: 380), meaning that social justice research can challenge social and institutional elitism, exclusion and prejudice. A social justice lens can uncover stories of marginalisation focusing on gender, race and class inequalities (Janesick, 2007) as well as other intersecting identities such as disability, gender identity, age, sexualities, Indigeneity, visa status, religion, ethnicity and language (Lenette, 2022). Social justice research prioritises methods that attend to the agendas and expertise of people who are often multiply marginalised.

Johnstone (2021: 637) argues that '[s]ocial injustice is always accompanied and underwritten by epistemic injustice, which supports and reinforces the dominant narrative', where epistemic injustice refers to instances where 'a person is wronged as a knower' (Fricker, 2010 in Johnstone, 2021: 635). There can be profound implications to being 'wronged' in this way because '[t]he capacity to reason and to give knowledge to others is fundamental to being human and so to be insulted or ignored in this capacity is deeply wounding' (Johnstone, 2021: 635). Ignoring or minimising lived experiences can result in ongoing epistemic injustice, and in some cases, epistemic violence, in the academy.

Lived experience-led knowledge can contribute to redressing the silences, erasures and perspective imbalances in the social justice literature. Janesick (2007: 116) sees the telling of stories in research as a social justice activity that gives those at the periphery an opportunity to 'refute myths, half truths, fabrications, and faulty perspectives'. The overall benefit of this approach is an increased awareness of social injustices and exposure to views that were previously missing. Janesick (2007: 119) concludes: 'As a social justice record is kept of stories from participants, most often marginalized in society, the stories become part of the historical record and, thus, the continuity of a society.' This further highlights the epistemic justice potential of lived experience-led knowledge.

Cook and colleagues (2019) argue that collective knowledge production is especially relevant to redressing social injustices. Several authors in this book provided community-oriented definitions of lived experience, which unsettle notions of top-down and individualistic expertise. Such models are ecological, grounded in the experiences and knowledge of individuals, families and the whole community, as well as environmental and social structures (see Vaioleti, 2013). For Atem Dau Atem (Chapter 6), wisdom gained from collective interpretation of lived experience in his Dinka community *determines* what reality is. Community-oriented understandings of lived experience are not uniformly reflexive and do not always account for all perspectives (Naufahu, 2018; Camminga, 2020), which is why intersectional analyses are crucial to explore such tensions.

While lived experience is a compelling form of knowledge in social justice research, an ongoing problem is that researchers can still misappropriate lived experience for their own gain (Costa et al, 2012). Those who research social injustices but have limited or no lived experience of these issues usually have the 'final word' on meaning-making and analysis and can continuously interpret, decontextualise or reimagine lived experience. They might not only lead people with first-hand experiences to underestimate their potential, but also tend to 'overestimate their cognitive powers and style themselves as intellectually superior' (Johnstone, 2021: 637).

As first-time editors, we reflected on how our approach differs from the very practices we critique and explain the author-led writing process in this chapter (we reflect on the challenges of our role in Chapter 9). All contributing authors felt that their chapters would be useful to researchers and people with similar lived experiences. But there are unresolved power imbalances in terms of how we (editors) benefit differently from this publication. Because of our academic privileges, our careers will no doubt be advantaged. We have worked closely with the authors to avoid being exploitative, so that they would benefit from the opportunity to exercise agency in how they wanted to share their knowledge. We continue to reflect on improving ethical models of collaborative writing in academia.

Further, we situate lived experience-led research as a specific model of participatory research. This approach positions people with lived experiences as co-researchers and co-producers of new knowledge (Cook et al, 2019; Penak and Allen, 2022), where 'people with direct experiences of, or interest in, the research topic participate in all or some aspects of the process, including research design, data, collection and analysis, and reporting and dissemination' (Lenette, 2022: 2). Co-research favours genuine and reciprocal collaboration, as well as contextualised and subjective knowledges that prioritise the agendas, perspectives and wishes of people with lived experiences (see Flinders et al, 2016). The emancipatory potential of participatory research points to its social justice aims (Cook et al, 2019). Co-creating new knowledge can redress the absence of first-hand experiences in the literature to improve the lives of co-researchers (see Lenette, 2022 for full discussion).

Importantly, as examples from this book demonstrate, lived experience-led knowledge goes well beyond addressing the limitations of social justice research to counter a much deeper problem: ideological beliefs that *deny the very existence of human beings* and their knowledge. When Uncle Stan Grant (Senior) and colleagues (Chapter 2) describe culturally centred and community-led processes that rebuild Wiradyuri nationhood, cultural renewal and strengthen identity, they respond directly to settler-colonisers' brutal attempts to erase Indigenous knowledges and languages for over 250 years through institutional and epistemic violence (see Vivian et al, 2017; Reid, 2020). The co-authors' collective reflections on their work and its wide-reaching impacts negate this erasure and re-value the intergenerational wisdom of Indigenous leaders. The oldest continuing living culture on the planet has survived and is still here despite ongoing institutional and epistemic violence (Reid, 2020).

Another example is Estelle Keerthana Ramaswamy's account as a Thirunangai (Tamil equivalent to transwoman) in Chapter 7. She contends with intersecting identities in a polemic trans-exclusionary feminist context that threatens her right to be a woman (see Camminga, 2020; Carrera-Fernàndez and DePalma, 2020) while often encountering culturally unsafe situations as an Indian-born PhD candidate living in Australia. When she is asked to refer to herself using a trans-exclusionary term ('trans woman' instead of transwoman), this imposition shows how language can deny her very existence and identity. South African trans scholar B Camminga (2020) discussed the dangers of semantics that can lead to and perpetuate violence (epistemic and physical) against transgender individuals when language is used recklessly. By resisting such demands (epistemic resistance) and using terms that align with her identity, Estelle Keerthana Ramaswamy exercises agency in framing her knowledge. She also challenges the lack of majority-world narratives of transgenderism where western-centric and white notions of gender and transgender identity set the agenda (see Camminga, 2020).

Lived experience-led methodologies

The chapter authors used four disruptive methodologies of knowledge production to share expertise based on lived experience: Indigenous nation building, *talanoa*, autoethnography and collaborative autoethnography. As you will see, their use of these methodologies counters tokenistic, performative, appropriative and exploitative approaches to the 'inclusion' of lived experience expertise.

Indigenous nation building supports Indigenous people and communities to decide what is important to them, what research should be undertaken and how it should be conducted. The approach prioritises culturally safe practices of deferring to Elders and 'explicitly concentrates on the return of knowledge, language, and culture to Indigenous peoples and on their revival within Indigenous communities' (Vivian et al, 2017: 53). In Chapter 2, Uncle Stan Grant (Senior) and colleagues describe how Indigenous nation building follows their community's ways of being, doing and knowing, which are difficult to translate into a western frame.

Talanoa is a culturally safe process for Pasifika researchers to share and hold a dialogical space to discuss social justice issues and support Pasifika communities (Vaioleti, 2013). It refers to 'a cultural synthesis of the information, stories and emotions for producing relevant knowledge and possibilities for addressing Pacific issues' (Naufahu, 2018: 17). In Chapter 8, Jioji Ravulo and colleagues describe how they used *talanoa* to uncover diverse and culturally nuanced perspectives and, in doing so, explicitly rejected the dominant western framing of lived experience research by adopting culturally safe and community-led approaches for their action and activism.

Autoethnography draws on the subjective to explore one's own experiences and involves 'embracing vulnerability with purpose' (Holman Jones et al, 2016: 22). Toyosaki and Pensoneau-Conway (2016: 560) describe autoethnography as 'the praxis of social justice' where researchers 'come to know (epistemology), evaluate (axiology), become (ontology), and do (praxiology) our selfhood – our sense of being – in the world'. As Chapters 3 and 7 best illustrate, autoethnographic approaches facilitate purposeful and intersectional critiques of research practices.

Collaborative autoethnography involves two or more researchers combining their lived experiences to engage in collaborative analysis and interpretation (Chang et al, 2016). This approach favours exploring complementary and contradictory experiences towards collective meaning-making to produce intersubjective and multivocal accounts that 'foster global collaboration [and] disrupt hegemonic theorizing' (Hernandez et al, 2017: 253). Different forms of collaborative autoethnography inform Chapters 4, 5, 6 and 8.

The lived experience-led knowledge presented in this book, whether sole- or collaboratively authored, points to the central importance of reflexivity to upend structures of accountability and recognition, and to recentre lived experience expertise. Reflexivity refers to researchers consciously reflecting on how their assumptions and positionalities shape research relationships, processes and outcomes, as an ethical imperative (Lenette, 2022). In each chapter, the authors are reflexive about their unique approaches in their own terms. This is an important principle that researchers across disciplines should adopt to truly realise the potential of lived experience-led knowledge.

Writing process

The knowledge in this book explicitly challenges outdated positionings of people with lived experiences that we observed in the academy for several years, including (1) representative positioning that can homogenise and diminish the interests and experiences of unique and diverse individuals; (2) guest positioning that reinforces people with lived experiences as 'other'; and (3) gatekeeper positioning that draws upon the knowledge and networks of people with lived experiences solely to legitimise dominant standpoints while under-acknowledging or ignoring their contributions to, and aspirations and goals for, research. To achieve this aim, authors focus explicitly on how they envision disruptive research and how their processes unsettle established norms of scholarly inquiry. The editing process promoted collaborative and reflexive knowledge co-creation and documentation, where authors could exercise agency in terms of how they wanted their perspectives to be represented.

Driven by our commitment to social justice, we did not impose a rigid pre-determined outline, which would contradict the ethos of co-produced knowledge. We only offered broad guidelines based on participatory research principles and processes. Transforming the academy requires that we change how we write. We agree with Alonso Bejarano and colleagues (2019) that we should move away from limiting forms of writing that cite the same 'experts' and use jargon to restrict audiences. A key example is Chapter 4, where the authors sought permission to write without an academic lead. They wanted the work to focus solely on their perspectives since other aspects of the project had not achieved that aim.

Of note, 'academic scholars and researchers' and 'people with lived experiences' are not mutually exclusive categories. This harmful binary has lost relevance (Costa et al, 2012; Fox, 2016; Moran et al, 2022). Some of the chapter authors have combined lived experience, scholarly expertise and the ability to bring these elements into social justice discourses through collaborative writing. We recognise that not everyone with relevant lived experiences will want to disclose that information, especially in academic contexts, often because of the labels, prejudices and stereotypes attached to those experiences.

We were also aware of the burden associated with taking a lead role to write for publication, especially when this was a completely new endeavour or not part of a paid role. We did not wish to create further inequities through our invitations to contribute. However, we found that (first-time) authors were strongly motivated to find the time to write and have discussions with co-authors, even when they had to relinquish personal time to complete this work. Being part of this initiative was a new way to exercise agency and consider the potential of their lived experience expertise to redress epistemic injustices. For some, this was the first time they reflected on their lived experiences and how to write about them.

Book structure

This book is organised into three parts. Part I, 'Theoretical grounding and underpinning values' sets the context for chapters that follow, by discussing culturally centred and community-led work to renew Indigenous ways of thinking and the importance of connecting with knowledge that has always been within (Chapter 2) and by critiquing current modes of engaging with lived experience expertise (Chapter 3). Part II, 'Scrutinising lived experience research processes through leadership and collaboration', critiques co-design research processes and issues of power, authority and expertise in research teams, through the perspectives of men who participated in a suicide prevention project in Australia (Chapter 4) and insights from collaborative research in Indonesia involving researchers with disability and disability service providers with no identified lived experience (Chapter 5). Part III, 'Decolonising lived experience research', illustrates how intersectional worldviews extend social justice research and the translation of decolonial approaches into research relationships, by discussing refugee-background and convict-coloniser descendent collaborations for ethical research (Chapter 6), via an autoethnographic account of a transwoman/transfemme researcher from India (Chapter 7), and through the perspectives of Pasifika community workers, leaders and researchers working with Pasifika communities in Australia (Chapter 8).

Chapter-by-chapter summaries

In Chapter 2, 'Examining for the purpose of knowing: Ngaabigi Winhangagigu', Uncle Stan Grant (Senior), Sue Green, Deb Evans, Donna Murray, Letitia Harris and Harry Lambshead demystify understandings of research beyond academic realms by drawing upon the Wiradyuri concepts of *ngaabinya* – examining, trying, attempting, testing, judging and evaluating, and *winhangagigu* – thinking, remembering and knowing. They outline Indigenous nation building as a powerful way to rebuild nationhood, cultural renewal and identity. The authors explain how culturally centred and community-led work is renewing Wiradyuri ways of thinking.

In Chapter 3, 'Towards a scholarship of Critical Lived Experience Engagement: big feelings, big stories, big learning', researcher, writer, artist and educator Rebecca J. Moran asks questions about lived experience engagement that have so far remained 'out of bounds' in the literature. Using an autoethnographic lens, she examines current modes of engaging with lived experience expertise and introduces the possibility of a scholarship of Critical Lived Experience Engagement.

In Chapter 4, 'Lived experience perspectives on a co-design process: the "Under the Radar" mens' suicide prevention project', Stephen Lake, Anonymous Lived Experience Advisors, Campbell Clerke, William Crompton, Norman Stevens, Ivan Ma, John O'Loughlin, Peter Sutton and Matt Whitten explore a common problem in participatory research: the lack of meaningful consideration of complex lived experiences when developing projects from outsider perspectives. Combining critical collective analysis of the co-design process with creative narratives, the authors reflect on their mental health struggles and experiences after attempting suicide, to problematise service delivery gaps. They discuss what could be done differently to better support Lived Experience Advisors in research.

In Chapter 5, 'Co-researching with persons with disabilities: reflections and lessons learned', Chrysant Lily Kusumowardoyo, Husna Yuni Wulansari, Irmansyah Songgoua, Elias Katapi, Zainab and Yassin Ali Hadu share experiences of co-research in a post-disaster context. Using reflective dialogue to problematise co-production practices, the authors share their assumptions, achievements and challenges in conducting community-led research. They highlight how entrenched privilege and power imbalances undermine relationships in collaborative partnerships and threaten full participation of co-researchers with disability.

In Chapter 6, 'Ethical and decolonial considerations of co-research in refugee studies: what are we missing?', Atem Dau Atem and Maree Higgins explore the ethics of relationship and the ethics of witnessing and documenting in co-research with people from refugee backgrounds. They critically assess current approaches, identifying homogenising and colonising tendencies in refugee studies then share their own experiences of research and collaboration using four vignettes.

In Chapter 7, 'Combating colonial pathologised universalisation: a transwoman's Indo-Australian lived experience', Estelle Keerthana Ramaswamy describes her experiences as a transwoman/transfemme from Chennai, India. She challenges the universalisation and homogenisation of sexual and gender diversity and trans and gender diverse lived experiences and describes how lived experience-led research in this field can be decolonised and disrupted.

In Chapter 8, 'Responding collaboratively to COVID-19 and our health needs across Pacific communities: CORE Pacific Collective', Jioji Ravulo, Seini Afeaki, Malaemie Fruean, Donina Va'a and Maherau Arona outline the *talanoa* process used to share and reflect on their experiences of working together to support Pasifika communities in Australia during the COVID-19 pandemic lockdowns. The authors highlight how culturally safe and community-led collaborations yielded effective health responses. They discuss the dynamic role of Pasifika Elders and the need to nurture *vā* (sacred spaces) with family and community through a whole-of-community and whole-of-government approach.

In Chapter 9, 'The potential of lived experience-led knowledge to dismantle the academy', we reiterate the disruptive and decolonial potentials of lived experience-led scholarship in social justice research and in the academy more broadly. We highlight the strengths of lived experience-led scholarship that no other research approach can replicate, as a lens that is unapologetically personal, inherently intersectional and undeniably visible.

Positionalities

Caroline

I am an uninvited first-generation migrant-settler living and working on unceded Aboriginal land since 2005. I am a woman with brown skin, making me a 'visible minority' in a white-majority country. English is my second language. While I experience discrimination based on my appearance, my gender and because I am a sole parent, my lived experiences differ greatly from that of the people I usually collaborate with in participatory research on forced migration. I have many privileges as an academic in a full-time, ongoing role, living in an affluent suburb and country. I am cisgender, non-disabled, middle-aged and a citizen of two countries.

I value participatory methodologies because of my commitment to social and gender justice and decolonising research, and because of the potential to change how we think about and conduct research to make it more respectful, ethical, trauma-informed and culturally safe. Recently, I became more aware of my complicity in perpetuating harmful approaches and recognised my unique standpoint and my moral and ethical responsibility as a migrant-settler woman scholar to decolonise research and the academy. My research activities and scholarship aim to decolonise practices that we barely question and that continue to result in harmful outcomes for people with complex lived realities and colleagues.

Maree

I am a cisgender, heterosexual, white woman, born in Australia of Irish heritage. My ancestors – convicts – brought to this land against their will, nevertheless participated in the colonisation and dispossession of these unceded Aboriginal lands, acts in which I remain complicit. While I have experienced vulnerability as a woman, a single mother and as a hospital inpatient – as a child for eye surgery, then again as a teenager after being hit by a car, and recently because of a serious fall – I have privilege due to my skin colour, education and access to safety, as well as opportunities not afforded to many around the world.

A social worker by background, I am employed as a social work researcher and educator. I am committed to applying decolonial approaches in teaching and research, finding Peggy McIntosh's (1989: 10) insights about white privilege useful: she describes skin privilege as 'an invisible weightless knapsack of special provisions, maps, passports, codebooks, visas, clothes, tools and blank checks' that constitute unearned life advantages about which I am conditioned to be oblivious. Recently, reflecting on my unearned advantages before a class, I noted a significant privilege that I often take for granted: "I can choose to practice in an area of social work where my lived experience is not central." This privilege has enabled me to work in many parts of the world and to co-create knowledge with people from refugee backgrounds. I value participatory methods because of my commitment to social justice and human rights from below and I am acutely conscious of my responsibility as a descendant of convict-colonisers and a woman scholar to explicitly apply decolonial principles in the research that I do.

Conclusion

The diversity of lived experience perspectives in this book speaks to different contexts and the intersectional nature of social justice issues, which are relevant to multiple disciplines. It is not possible, nor useful, to reduce the contextual challenges of disrupting academic practices, decolonising social justice research and achieving epistemic justice to a simple tick-box approach. This is why we have privileged intersectional perspectives in the chapters that follow.

In the process of editing the chapters, we have not 'sanitised' lived experience accounts to fit pre-determined models of academic scholarship. The chapter authors chose how they wanted to present their perspectives. We hope that the book's format does justice to the contributors' narratives in all their complexity and richness. We recognise that there are still limitations in terms of who will read, engage with and value this content. There is more to do to disrupt and decolonise the academy. We hope that the book contributes to much-needed dialogue on social justice research and the under-recognised value and potentials of lived experience-led knowledge.

Note
[1]   We deliberately use lower case 'w' in 'white' to disrupt colonialist and hegemonic academic discourses.

Further reading

The Critical Methodologies Collective (2022) *The Politics and Ethics of Representation in Qualitative Research: Addressing Moments of Discomfort*, London: Taylor & Francis.

Faulkner, A. and Thompson, R. (2021) 'Uncovering the emotional labour of involvement and co-production in mental health research', *Disability & Society*, 38(4): 537–560.

Kusumowardoyo, C.L. and Wulansari, H.Y. (2022) 'Towards meaningful participation in humanitarian studies: Co-researching with persons with disabilities in Central Sulawesi', *Disaster Prevention and Management*, 31(2): 158–165.

Seppälä, T., Sarantou, M. and Miettinen, S. (eds) (2021) *Arts-Based Methods for Decolonising Participatory Research*, Oxfordshire: Routledge.

References

Alonso Bejarano, C., López Juárez, L., Mijangos García, M.A. and Goldstein, D.M. (2019) *Decolonizing Ethnography: Undocumented Immigrants and New Directions in Social Science*, Durham, NC: Duke University Press.

Álvarez, L. and Coolsaet, B. (2020) 'Decolonizing environmental justice studies: A Latin American perspective', *Capitalism Nature Socialism*, 31(2): 50–69.

Barnacle, R. (2004) 'Reflection on lived experience in educational research', *Educational Philosophy and Theory*, 36(1): 57–67.

Black Dog Institute (2023) Aboriginal and Torres Strait Islander Lived Experience Centre. Available from: https://www.blackdoginstitute.org.au/education-services/aboriginal-and-torres-strait-islander-network/ [Accessed 1 June 2023].

Camminga, B (2020) 'Disregard and danger: Chimamanda Ngozi Adichie and the voices of trans (and cis) African feminists', *The Sociological Review*, 68(4): 817–833.

Carrera-Fernández, M.V. and DePalma, R. (2020) 'Feminism will be trans-inclusive or it will not be: Why do two cis-hetero woman educators support transfeminism?', *The Sociological Review*, 68(4): 745–762.

Chang, H., Ngunjiri, F. and Hernandez, K.A.C. (2016) *Collaborative Autoethnography*, London and New York: Routledge.

Cook, T., Brandon, T., Zonouzi, M. and Thomson, L. (2019) 'Destabilising equilibriums: Harnessing the power of disruption in participatory action research', *Educational Action Research*, 27(3): 379–395.

Costa, L., Voronka, J., Landry, D., Reid, J., McFarlane, B., Reville, D. and Church, K. (2012) 'Recovering our stories: A small act of resistance', *Studies in Social Justice*, 6(1): 85–101.

Dorozenko, K.P., Ridley, S., Martin, R. and Mahboub, L. (2016) 'A journey of embedding mental health lived experience in social work education', *Social Work Education*, 35(8): 905–917.

Flinders M., Wood, M. and Centre, C. (2016) 'The politics of co-production: Risks, limits and pollution', *Evidence and Policy*, 12(2): 261–279.

Fox, J. (2016) 'Being a service user and a social work academic: Balancing expert identities', *Social Work Education*, 35(8): 960–969.

Ginsberg, F. and Rapp, R. (2020) 'Disability/anthropology: Rethinking the parameters of the human. An introduction to supplement 21', *Current Anthropology*, 61(21): S4–15.

Hage, G. (1999) *White Nation: Fantasies of White Supremacy in a Multicultural Society*, Sydney: Pluto Press.

Hernandez, K.A.C., Chang, H. and Ngunjiri, F.W. (2017) 'Collaborative autoethnography as multivocal, relational, and democratic research: Opportunities, challenges, and aspirations', *a/b: Auto/Biography Studies*, 32(2): 251–254.

Holman Jones, S., Adams, T.E. and Ellis, C. (2016) *Handbook of Autoethnography*, Oxon and New York: Routledge.

Janesick, V.J. (2007) 'Oral history as a social justice project: Issues for the qualitative researcher', *The Qualitative Report*, 12(1): 111–121.

Johnstone, M. (2021) 'Centering social justice in mental health practice: Epistemic justice and social work practice', *Research on Social Work Practice*, 31(6): 634–643.

Kamwaria, A. and Katola, M. (2012) 'The role of African traditional religion, culture and world-view in the context of post-war healing among the Dinka community of Southern Sudan', *International Journal of Humanities and Social Science*, 2(21): 49–55.

Kara, H. (2022) 'The value and limitations of lived experience', *Helen Kara Blog Post*. Available from: https://helenkara.com/2022/07/14/the-value-and-limitations-of-lived-experience/ [Accessed 30 October 2022].

Lenette, C. (2022) *Participatory Action Research: Ethics and Decolonization*, New York: Oxford University Press.

Mahmud, L. (2021) 'Feminism in the house of anthropology', *Annual Review of Anthropology*, 50(1): 345–361.

Mathers, L.A.B., Sumerau, J.E. and Cragun, R.T. (2018) 'The limits of homonormativity: Constructions of bisexual and transgender people in the post-gay era', *Sociological Perspectives*, 61(6): 934–952.

McIntosh, P. (1989) 'White privilege: Unpacking the invisible knapsack', *Peace and Freedom Magazine*, July/August: 10–12.

Moosavi, L. (2020) 'The decolonial bandwagon and the dangers of intellectual decolonisation', *International Review of Sociology*, 30(2): 332–354.

Moran, R.J., Martin, R. and Ridley, S. (2022) '"It helped me open my eyes": Incorporating lived experience perspectives in social work education', *Affilia*, 1–16.

Naufahu, M. (2018) 'A Pasifika research methodology: Talaloto', *Waikato Journal of Education*, 23(1): 15–24.

Penak, N. and Allen, R. (2022) 'Beyond "indigenous social work" and toward decolonial possibility: Stories from Toronto's Red Road', *Intersectionalities: A Global Journal of Social Work Analysis, Research, Polity, and Practice*, 10(1): 1–18.

Reid, T. (2020) '2020: The year of reckoning, not reconciliation', *Griffith Review 67 Matters of Trust*. Available from: https://www.griffithreview.com/articles/2020-year-of-reckoning/ [Accessed 18 June 2023].

Rigney, D., Bignall, S., Vivian, A. and Hemming, S. (2022) *Indigenous Nation Building and the Political Determinants of Health and Wellbeing: Discussion Paper*, Melbourne: Lowitja Institute.

Ryan, N.E. and El Ayadi, A.M (2020) 'A call for a gender-responsive, intersectional approach to address COVID-19', *Global Public Health*, 15(9): 1404–1412.

Simpson, A. (2017) 'The ruse of consent and the anatomy of "refusal": Cases from indigenous North America and Australia', *Postcolonial Studies*, 20(1): 18–33.

Toyosaki, S. and Pensoneau-Conway, S.L. (2016) 'Autoethnography as a praxis of social justice: Three ontological contexts', in S. Holman Jones, T.E. Adams and C. Ellis (eds) *Handbook of Autoethnography*, Oxon and New York: Routledge, pp 557–575.

Tuck, E. (2009) 'Suspending damage: A letter to communities', *Harvard Educational Review*, 79(3): 409–428.

Tuck, E. and Yang, K.W. (2012) 'Decolonization is not a metaphor', *Decolonization: Indigeneity, Education & Society*, 1(1): 1–40.

Tuhiwai Smith, L.T. (2021) *Decolonizing Methodologies: Research and Indigenous Peoples* (3rd edn), London: Zed Books.

Vaioleti, T. (2013) 'Talanoa: Differentiating the talanoa research methodology from phenomenology, narrative, Kaupapa Maori and feminist methodologies', *Reo, Te*, 56: 191–212.

Vivian, A., Jorgensen, M., Cornell, S., Rigney, D., Hemming, S. and Bell, D. (2017) 'Enlivening Indigenous methodologies in Indigenous public policy research', *Ngiya: Talk the Law*, 5: 47–74.

Wane, N.N. (2006) 'Is decolonization possible?', in G.J.S. Dei and A. Kempf (eds) *Anti-Colonialism and Education: The Politics of Resistance*, Leiden: Brill, pp 87–106.

Watego, C. (2021) *Another Day in the Colony*, Brisbane: University of Queensland Press.

Watego, C., Whop, L.J., Singh, D., Mukandi, B., Macoun, A., Newhouse, G., Drummond, A., McQuire, A., Stajic, J., Kajlich, H. and Brough, M. (2021) 'Black to the future: Making the case for indigenist health humanities', *International Journal of Environmental Research and Public Health*, 18(8704): 1–10.

Williams, R. (1999) 'Cultural safety: What does it mean for our work practice?', *Australian and New Zealand Journal of Public Health*, 23(2): 213–214.

Wright, S. and Patrick, R. (2019) 'Welfare conditionality in lived experience: Aggregating qualitative longitudinal research', *Social Policy and Society*, 18(4): 597–613.

PART I

Theoretical grounding and underpinning values

2

Examining for the purpose of knowing: Ngaabigi Winhangagigu

Uncle Stan Grant (Senior), Sue Green, Deb Evans, Donna Murray, Letitia Harris and Harry Lambshead

Key points

- This chapter disrupts the academy by demystifying research *by*, *for* and *with* Indigenous peoples, recognising the ability of people at the grassroots to undertake serious research into areas, topics or issues that are important and of priority to them.
- Wiradyuri *buyaa* (law) demands that Wiradyuri people must listen to the wisdom of their wise Elders. The success of working in this way is evident in the story of the multi-award-winning Graduate Certificate in Wiradjuri Language, Culture and Heritage from Charles Sturt University, which is a body of work undertaken by community spirited Wiradyuri Elders, and others they co-opted to support their vision.
- The Wiradjuri Language, Culture and Heritage Course applies an Indigenous nation building methodology, which views the language and wisdom traditions of our Ancestors as foundational assets for securing vibrant and positive futures for our people and allows us to build upon and continue working in the ways we have for time immemorial.
- Ngaabigi winhangaguigu or, in English, 'research', only exists in its relationship with the researcher.

Introduction

This chapter is based upon culturally centred and community-led research. It is culturally centred because it is grounded within and conducted through Wiradyuri cultural practices, including deferring to Elders, working collaboratively and ensuring respect towards all others. A significant part of Wiradyuri cultural practices is to ensure that the community decide what is important, that is, what research should be undertaken and how it should be conducted.

Research is not something that belongs exclusively in the academic or professional world, where only the experts (researchers) have the ability to undertake research. In the field of research *by*, *for* and *with* Indigenous peoples, it is critical that research is demystified and that people at the grassroots are recognised as having the ability to undertake serious research into areas, topics or issues that are important and of priority to them. Vivian and colleagues (2017) refer to this approach as the Indigenous nation building methodology. This approach allows Indigenous nations to build upon and to continue working in the ways they have for time immemorial. Wiradyuri[1] are rebuilding their nation by strengthening their communities to be places where their 'children can live *yindyamarra*'.

Wiradyuri are one of over 250 different First Nations language groups within the country now called Australia. The Wiradyuri Nation is located in Central Western New South Wales. Wiradyuri people continue to exist and live on their Country despite the ongoing effects and efforts of colonisation to remove them. Wiradyuri people still hold and practise their culture and beliefs today. Wiradyuri *buyaa* (law) demands that Wiradyuri people must listen to the wisdom of their wise Elders. The success of working in this way is evident in the story of the multi-award-winning Graduate Certificate of Wiradjuri Language, Culture and Heritage from Charles Sturt University, which is a body of work undertaken by key community spirited Wiradyuri Elders, and others they co-opted to support their vision (Charles Sturt University 2023a). Today, they continue to actively research with the purpose of rebuilding the language and wisdom traditions of their Ancestors as a foundational asset for securing vibrant and positive futures for their people.

It is truly remarkable work. It demonstrates a powerful way to rebuild Wiradyuri nationhood, cultural renewal and strengthen identity. Wiradyuri people are finding their own ways of recovering from colonisation and dispossession in all sorts of diverse spaces. They hope others can be energised and inspired to find their own paths as Wiradyuri have done. Of course, it will need to be different, it will need to be grounded in the very communities which the work serves, it will need community spirited Elders who have the cultural authority and legitimacy, it will require community spirited leaders, ethical, community-based researchers and change makers who have a shared vision for the greater good of the nation, connected to the grassroots, who are predominately from those respective nations and communities.

Interestingly, the work includes an examination of, and deeper connection to, the Wiradyuri Cosmology. Despite attempts of settler-colonialism to replace Wiradyuri ways, this Cosmology is not frozen in time or limited to origin stories of the universe and explaining the structure of the natural world. It is also a complex understanding of a system of Wiradyuri *buyaa* through which all identities, all relationships, all actions, all focus and all transformations exist (Grant and Rudder, 2014). The entire language system sits within these five categories, as outlined in Figure 2.1 (Green et al, 2020).

Figure 2.1: Wiradyuri Cosmology

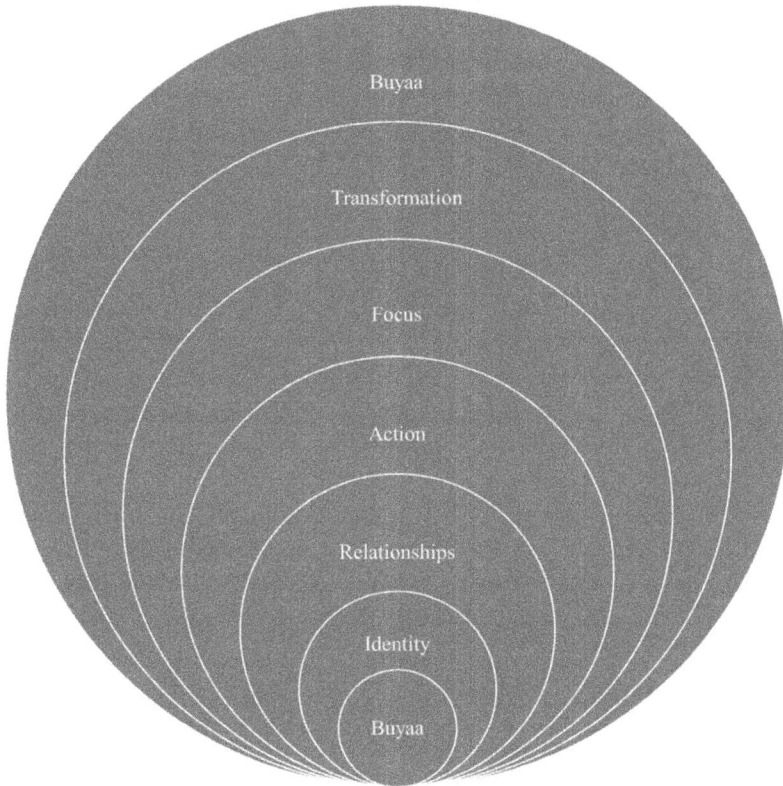

Today, this Cosmology is transforming the teaching and learning work within the Wiradjuri Language, Culture and Heritage Course. While it sits in stark contrast to western philosophical understandings of the world, Wiradyuri people are examining their own knowledge systems in a bid to solve their own problems, and determine, for themselves, futures of their own design.

So why has this culturally centred and community-led work been so successful in renewing Wiradyuri ways of thinking, and is it relevant or appropriate in these modern times and circumstances? Why not just all speak English? Wiradyuri language carries Wiradyuri ways of understanding the world. Wiradyuri *buyaa* carries a specialness that reminds Wiradyuri people about what it truly means to be from this land, what being Wiradyuri means at a deeper 'inside' level. Luckily, it can also act as a reminder to all of humanity as to what it means to act as grown-ups, to act as people who are responsible for the generations yet to come, a reminder of what it takes to leave the world better than we found it. Wiradyuri language makes Wiradyuri people, Wiradyuri. It orientates people accordingly, it supports the expression of how to live as citizens who are responsible, dependable, as it carries our ways of thinking, our ways of being and our Wiradyuri actions. These are all critical aspects of coming to embody *yindyamarra* and living according to Wiradyuri *buyaa*. Wiradyuri often loses much of its meaning when translated into English. Central to being Wiradyuri is knowing how to relate to all other things; Wiradyuri place names and cultural concepts for how to live a good Wiradyuri life are embodied within the language itself. This is why English can complement Wiradyuri but never replace it.

Yindyamarra winhanganha (Grant et al, 2015), which loosely translates to the 'wisdom of respectfully knowing how to live well, in a world worth living in', has been adopted by Charles Sturt University (2023b). This Wiradyuri phrase is thought to encapsulate the philosophy of how people should live and what they should aspire to. *Yindyamarra winhanganha* is grounded in ways of respectfully knowing that allowed the university to articulate their vision for their staff and students.

However, the entire Wiradyuri language and ways of thinking, knowing and understanding the world have the potential to unify their people and ease the trauma caused by settler-colonial practices. This can also allow all people living and working on Wiradyuri Country the capacity to transform practices and act like responsible grown-ups who are part of the natural world, not separate or superior to it. This work stands on the shoulders of the wisdom traditions of those who have come before them and picks up on the intergenerational wisdom that has been passed on through the language and lifeways of their Ancestors. This, Wiradyuri people believe, will heal their Country and their people. This is an intergenerational story that is central to healing and transforming their capacity as Wiradyuri people to live well, in a Wiradyuri world worth living in. Wiradyuri people are determined to solve their own problems because they know that colonial governments cannot do it for them.

For Wiradyuri people, research is not about discovering something new, but rather, about remembering what already exists and has always been known. In Wiradyuri Cosmology, nothing has ever not existed, and nothing ever ceases to exist (Grant and Rudder, 2014). It is just that it needs to be rediscovered and brought back into the outside world as a way of reorientating Wiradyuri people back to the wisdom traditions of their Ancestors. Significant Wiradyuri knowledge and lifeways have 'gone inside' because of the policies and practices of settler-colonialism. Research into the deeper and highly complex system of Wiradyuri knowledge is ensuring people start to act like grown-ups, be responsible citizens of the planet, and lead for the greater good of the Wiradyuri collective. They live to fulfil their Wiradyuri obligations and responsibilities as the First Peoples of Wiradyuri lands and waters and bring Wiradyuri wisdom traditions to the forefront.

Wiradyuri Elders and researchers are re-establishing the systems and spaces in which Wiradyuri people can once again be reorientated according to the wise ways of their Ancestors. This, they believe, allows them to secure futures of their own Wiradyuri design and ensure their young people can live according to their own Wiradyuri dreams and aspirations.

Hence, research is about the process of *ngaabinya* – of examining, trying, attempting, testing, judging, and evaluating, in order to *winhangagigu* – to think, remember and know. This is the process that Wiradyuri people have been going through for over 30 years now to restore their language and their place as the sovereign people of the Wiradyuri Nation. In the words of Uncle Stan Grant (Senior), 'We are healing our language to heal our people' (Grant, 2022). In healing our language, we heal Country, and in healing Country, we are healing all else including people. To rebuild the Wiradyuri Nation, we must have healthy Country and people, as all things are interconnected, and none exist separately to the other.

Wiradyuri Country and people have always existed and have always existed together. Wiradyuri people do not believe they migrated from other parts of the world, they are part of Country and exist within Country. Wiradyuri Country and people were always strong and healthy until the devastating events of settler-colonialism. In 1813, the first invaders, three British men, Blaxland, Wentworth and Lawson, crossed the Mountains into Wiradyuri Country (Gapps, 2021), thus beginning a time of great disruption to Wiradyuri life. Since then, Wiradyuri people have fought to preserve their way of life and to protect Country. The invaders have attempted to strip everything from Wiradyuri people: their land, their language and their identity. The colonisers also attempted to strip everything from Country, taking away her identity, her language and her *buyaa*. They aimed to wipe out Wiradyuri people and to dominate Country. However, Wiradyuri people and Country have survived and are now in a period of Restoration.

In order to tell the story of Restoration, the rest of this chapter is broken up into the voices of a number of Wiradyuri people and their allies. The sections are in the voices of those who are telling their part of the story. By no means does this chapter contain all voices, rather, it focuses on four graduates, and their stories take you on the journey of how they became involved – as the Restoration is as much about the strengths of individual people as the collective efforts of the Nation. Each of these people have been involved in *ngaabigi winhangagigu* (research) in working to restore Wiradyuri language and consciously working towards rebuilding the Wiradyuri Nation.

We cannot start telling our individual stories without first acknowledging and honouring the work of Uncle Dr Stan Grant (Member of the Order of Australia) who is a senior Wiradyuri Elder who received national recognition from his own people when he won the prestigious National Aboriginal and Islander Day Observance Committee Lifetime Achievement Award in 2022 for his tireless work to renew the ancestral language of his people. Remarkably, Uncle Stan's language knowledge remains central to how he lives his life, and the work he does to re-orientate his people for them to live a 'proper' Wiradyuri life. To him, being 'properly Wiradyuri' means to live according to Wiradyuri *buyaa*; getting to know Wiradyuri Cosmology from a deeper insider's perspective, he hopes, will be a unifying feature from which to rebuild the individual and collective capacity of his people to live *yindyamarra*, to live a gentle and respectful life. For Uncle Stan, despite it being illegal, somehow, he managed to learn directly from his grandfather, Budyaan Wilfred Johnson, who was jailed for speaking to his grandson in Wiradyuri. Fast-forward approximately 70 years and along with his non-Indigenous brother, Dr John Rudder, Uncle Stan has undertaken remarkable work in reclaiming the Wiradyuri language, which has led to the development of the multiple-award-winning Graduate Certificate of Wiradjuri Language, Culture and Heritage at Charles Sturt University under the direction of Wiradyuri Elders and other nation builders.

Uncle Stan's story

I grew up in a period when my language, the Wiradyuri language, was outlawed. I saw my grandfather jailed for speaking the language to his grandchildren. However, our language never went away. As time passed, our language was no longer outlawed but very few people knew the language and many only had a few words and were no longer fluent speakers. One day, someone gave my sister, Florence, a document containing Wiradyuri language, which had been written by a white person. Florence and our brother, Wongama, started looking at this document and knew that we could work on restoring our language. Wongama and the other old Elders told me that it was my responsibility to revive our language and teach it to our people. At first, I was resistant, as I didn't believe that I would be able to carry such a responsibility. However, my brother and sister insisted and, thus, I began my journey of restoring our language.

The job of restoring the language involved spending many hours, days and years researching our language. Along the way, I was introduced to Dr John Rudder, a Christian missionary and academic, who became my brother. Together, we researched the Wiradyuri language and then travelled extensively across Wiradyuri Country to teach the language of my Wiradyuri Ancestors. We complied the Wiradyuri Dictionaries and Grammar Book (Grant and Rudder, 2010; Grant and Rudder, 2014), along with numerous recordings, other workbooks and teaching resources.

Wongama, Florence and myself, along with a group of people including the original Wiradyuri Council of Elders and Deb and Donna who speak next, started thinking about how we could get more sustainable pathways and we were fortunate enough to have some good friends and allies who worked at Charles Sturt University. Together, we developed and implemented the Graduate Certificate of Wiradjuri Language, Culture and Heritage. In 2014, we had our first intake of 19 students with myself, John Rudder, Ros Brennan Kemmis, Deb Evans (and others) teaching. In that inaugural cohort of students, we were fortunate to have Letetia Harris and Harry Lambshead (who speak later), who demonstrated not only the depth of their Wiradyuri language speaking skills but also how to teach language. By the time Letetia and Harry completed their course, they were teaching the next intake of students. Today, everyone who works on the course is a graduate of the course.

Deb and Donna's story

Wiradyuri Nation has the largest cultural footprint in New South Wales and extends across the rich riverine mountains, rivers, plains and valleys. Its diversity, richness and beauty are reflected in the estimated tens of thousands Wiradyuri citizens who live on and off Country.

I (Donna) am Wiradyuri with kinship connections to our people of the Murrumbidga (Murrumbidgee) and Galari (Lachlan) rivers. Growing up on Country provided me the opportunity to know, spend time, listen and learn from our old people and extended family, although as a young person, hearing my grandfather's and father's yarns, I didn't really understand the significance of storytelling.

I (Deb) am a Malyangapa/Ngiyampaa *wiimpatja* from Far Western New South Wales who loves returning home regularly. I have lived and worked on Wiradyuri Country since 1994 and am thankful for my deep connections with Wongama, Pastor Cec Grant (deceased), Uncle Dr Stan Grant and several other key Wiradyuri Elders, many of whom still guide me given I am living and working on someone else's Country. I am passionate about renewing language, and Indigenous nation rebuilding as a way of recovering our cultural lifeways in order to live according to our own Indigenous worldview.

As the stars aligned on Wiradyuri Nation, we found each other with a shared vision and passion for our people through education and community development initiatives. We became great friends, colleagues and family over the past 25 years. Along the way, in the late 1990s, we were very privileged to spend time working with Uncle Cec Grant (Wongama) who was a strong Wiradyuri leader, mentor and visionary, who took us under his mentorship, often saying that he could see something in the way we worked that was going to be a game-changer into the future. He would say "You're not listening with your eyes, ears and cultural heart" and was frustrated when we struggled to understand Wiradyuri ways and concepts that he was so generously sharing with us, with a specific purpose but without telling us the purpose!

After a few years of sharing knowledge, building our leadership capacity, and gaining insight into his 'purpose', Wongama finally stated, "All I want is for you two to rebuild the nation!", and today, we are honouring that gift of responsibility that he gave us all those years ago with passion, commitment and courage. In 2011–2012, we met another profoundly important mentor, Professor Miriam Jorgenson, from Arizona's Native Nations Institute, and collaborated to run a series of 'changing the conversation' initiatives. The collaboration was further enhanced when we met Dr Alison Vivian, from the University of Technology Sydney's Indigenous Nations and Collaborative Futures Hub. These two Indigenous nation building methodology researchers profoundly transformed our thinking and our work and our students of the Wiradjuri Language, Culture and Heritage Course continue to benefit from this long-standing collaboration.

Today, this interdisciplinary team is working to rebuild the Wiradyuri Nation in partnership with Wiradyuri people, grounded in Wiradyuri ways of knowing, being and doing. Our work is firmly centred around Uncle Stan Grant's life's work to revitalise the Wiradyuri language in a deep conceptual way that transforms the thinking, feelings and actions of Wiradyuri citizens and other non-Wiradyuri allies who are living and working on Wiradyuri Country.

Attending the nation building programme (referred to as 'January in Tucson'), an intensive programme that brings together experts in Indigenous governance and Indigenous rights to provide a space for important dialogue between Indigenous peoples based on 30 years of Harvard evidence, gave us a lens from which to secure a self-determining process, and begin changing the conversation and reversing over two centuries of trauma (University of Arizona, 2022). This resulted in us being strategically focused on conducting community-based research that allowed us to undertake a series of conversations that built a basis for researching, trialling and testing the tools and strategies from the Harvard/Native Nations Institute research, but adapted for use within our Wiradyuri context. What became evident was that Indigenous nation building has always been there within our ways, as future-based thinking is one of our custodianship responsibilities. We have been able to develop a research methodology that is based on Wiradyuri cultural values and ways of living, which are demonstrated by *yindyamarra* (respect and honour), *bagaraybang* (to restore, and make comfortable and healthy), *yindyamarra winhanganha* and *muwugamarra* (keep in reserve for future use).

While this work provides a useful paradigm shift for the Aboriginal shared space, it is critical for Wiradyuri people to be able to rebuild the Wiradyuri Nation to protect Wiradyuri custodianship responsibilities. It allows Wiradyuri to be self-determining in how they develop relationships with other Indigenous nations, and with settler-colonial governments to ensure the social, cultural, economic and environmental development for Wiradyuri people and the Wiradyuri Nation. For non-Indigenous people who work with Wiradyuri as allies, it allows them to ensure that they are not contributing to the western dominant cultural worldview that is replicated through the power relationships that exist within institutions where research traditionally occurs, such as universities. For those seeking to work with and alongside Wiradyuri people, they must respect and embed cultural responsiveness into their daily practice. Their actions must include honouring nation-specific cultural values, ways of working, ways of knowing, being and doing, led by Wiradyuri people, by, for and with Wiradyuri people, where the Wiradyuri Nation and Nation structures drive the priorities, aspirations and decision-making on Wiradyuri terms. This includes acknowledging and valuing the Nation's collective identity and finding solutions that are sustainable, just and democratic. The strength is in Wiradyuri culture, identity, relationships, kinship, Country, and land, as determined by the Nation citizens.

We continue our nation building work through workshops, summits and research with and within Wiradyuri and other First Peoples nation rebuilding projects. We also work closely with the staff of the Wiradjuri Language, Culture and Heritage Course. This involves us teaching into the subject on Rebuilding Australia's Indigenous Nations and being involved in developing new material and content. Furthermore, we work as part of the team along with Letetia, Harry and Sue (whose stories follow) in reflecting upon and researching the deeper meanings contained within Wiradyuri Cosmology, language and ways of being. In finishing our part of the story in this chapter, we want to pay our respects to all the Wiradyuri Elders who have and continue to lead this Wiradyuri nation building work that is rebuilding a strong, collective Wiradyuri Nation for the generations yet to come.

Today we are all part of a multidisciplinary team of people who teach, write and research in relation to Wiradyuri language and/or Indigenous nation building in the hope that it might energise and inspire others.

Teish and Yarri's story

Yiradhu marang, bala-dhu guyal dharran-giyalang. Ngadhu yali-nyal badhiin-gu-bu babiin-gu-bu ngiyang. Yuwin-dhu Yaladidya. Bala-dhu Wiradyuri! (Good day, I belong to Cooyal Creek. I speak to you in the language of my grandmother and father. My name is Letetia. I am Wiradyuri!)

I have been taught my language as an adult by my Elders and have been able to do this by the work they have done in reclaiming and teaching our language. I have been grown in Wiradyuri language teaching, learning to teach beside them and instructed by them. I continue to work under the instruction of my Elders to revitalise Wiradyuri language for our Nation.

The Wiradyuri Nation has access to their language because of the work of these Elders.

I did not grow up speaking my language fluently. I only knew static words that I used as a child/teenager from the Cowra community. I remember distinctly the first time that I heard Wiradyuri language spoken fluently. I was 19 years old, working as an Aboriginal Education Assistant in St Clare's College. I had invited Uncle Stan Grant (Senior) to come to the school as guest to speak to the Year 9 English class. Uncle Stan was friends with my father and uncle. I stood in front of the class ready to introduce Uncle Stan, but he directed me to sit down behind him. He then turned to the class and spoke fluently in Wiradyuri. I was overwhelmed with a wave of connection and belonging. Hearing our language. The language of my Ancestors. The language of my Country. His voice was like a memory in my spirit. And what he spoke was felt in every essence of my being. I knew it somehow, it was who I am, it was my identity, my truth. This fanned a fire that I didn't know was burning. It took another six years before the Elders and Ancestors found me grown enough to hold this knowledge with the respect it deserved. I was fortunate enough to live in and be part of a community where people were teaching and learning Wiradyuri language.

In 2007, along came Yindyamarra, my son. Being named Yindyamarra for doing things respectfully, politely, softly, gave him a lot to live up to and me too. Because of all of the work and knowledge my Elders had invested in me, I was able to speak to my son in Wiradyuri from birth, teaching him in his language, his truth. Restoring the ways of my Ancestors.

Baladhu Wiradyuri-giyalang gurawalar-i gunhinarrung-gu ngurambang. Yuwindhu Yarri (I be Wiradyuri belonging from Koorawatha, my grandmother's country. My name is Harry). Edna May Gilbert, her country *bala* (be) Boobaroy Euabalong, New South Wales. My grandmother and my mother Gloria Lambshead are the mothers who placed me and told me I am Wiradyuri.

My language journey commenced when I was a baby through my mothers, speaking words to me. However, as I grew older, I moved away from practising my culture until a workplace injury, which gave me the opportunity to re-evaluate my life.

The first words spoken to me were a mixture of English and Wiradyuri. So, I grew up with words of Wiradyuri but not sentences. Words like *bubul, guwaan, nginggi, mugiiny, ngarabang* and *yaambul*. These words were spoken to me at home and in my school years. After leaving school, my language went off the radar, so to speak. I had a very busy time working and completing an apprenticeship in the bricklaying/building trade which slowed my connections to my language, Wiradyuri ngiyang. There were many years where I was disconnected from my culture. Following an injury to my back caused by many years of bricklaying, I had to reassess what to do with my life.

My family suggested that I do a leadership programme, a certificate in Indigenous Leadership at Technical College. My teacher was an Aboriginal woman from Alice Springs who was able to speak her language and spoke with such passion. It was at this point that I began actively perusing my language. I managed to find that my language, Wiradyuri language, was being taught at Technical College in Dubbo, New South Wales. I undertook a certificate in Wiradyuri language and was taught by Aunty Beth Wright. It was during this time that I became hooked on learning language for life. I then began a course in Wiradyuri language which was being taught at Technical College in Dubbo. I became hooked on learning my language, which has become my lifelong journey now. At this time, while I was working at Cowra High School as an Aboriginal Education Officer, I met a young lady called Letetia. It was as if my Ancestors were guiding me on my journey. Letetia is a Wiradyuri woman who could speak Wiradyuri in a fluent way. Letetia's support and guidance in teaching me how to pronounce and speak my language has catapulted me to be a proud and confident Wiradyuri man who can speak his language. Letetia convinced me to teach.

Four years later, I (Letetia) moved back to Cowra. It is there that I met Harry while working at Cowra High School. It took no time for Harry to discover that I spoke our language and my relationship with Uncle Stan Grant. This prompted many impromptu lessons and eventuated in me teaching some high school classes in Wiradyuri. Harry was a natural with Wiradyuri language. I often commented to Uncle Stan how he sounded like him. I soon convinced Harry to teach with me and I will never look back. He made my teaching better, two peas in a pod, we became a teaching team. Our commitment to our language, our people and Elders was always at the forefront. We lit spot fires wherever we taught with language. We, as always, taught where we were told to. Under the instruction of Uncle Stan and local Elders, we taught at Cowra High School, Young High School, and at Technical Colleges in Tumut, Young and Cowra.

Uncle Stan instructed us to study and complete the Wiradjuri Language, Culture and Heritage Course. Harry and I did this together. Then we were instructed to teach Language in the Wiradjuri Graduate Certificate. Now, under the continuing guidance of Uncle Stan, we are at the next stage of our language journey; while still teaching at Charles Sturt University, we along with Sue (whose story follows) and two of our graduates, are undertaking a course in Linguistics at Batchelor Institute in the Northern Territory. This will allow us to have the skills to continue the work of Uncle Stan and Dr John Rudder in being able to interpret the work of those early linguists who recorded Wiradyuri language.

Our language, Wiradyuri *ngiyang*, is waking up and living, it is alive on our Country, *ngiyanhigingu ngurambang*. This is seen through all the work of Uncle Stan in the production of many books including the Wiradyuri

Dictionary (Grant and Rudder, 2010), grammar book (Grant and Rudder, 2014), videos and children's books. The resources for our community are priceless: they keep our language alive. They support knowledge holders to produce more resources like Wiradyuri cartoons, video translations and voice overs, renaming of streets and places, and the understanding of those names are being welcomed by towns and communities. Language has the power to draw you in. It locates you; it gives you strength, belonging and connection.

We believe in the strong, respectful way that Uncle Stan Grant leads our people and guides his teachers through the teaching of *yindyamarra*. Taking language into our community gives people strength and pride and has the power to uplift and direct people in the right direction. We acknowledge all those who work and teach alongside in the language programme, particularly Elders such Uncle Stan, Aunty Elaine Lomas and Uncle Pat Connelly.

Sue's story

Yuwindhu Dyudyan (My name is Sue). My family has experienced generations of being denied access to our language and our culture which has included the experience of child removal for myself and my siblings. Growing up, I always knew I was Aboriginal but not until I found my father in my mid-20s did I know that I was Wiradyuri. It was a long, slow journey to discovering my Wiradyuriness. At the time I found my father, I also decided to start university studies. I had extremely poor access to formal schooling and thus a low level of educational attainment. University study opened the door to so many opportunities for myself and my children. I returned to Sydney and commenced the Bachelor of Social Work in 1995 after being taken as a child from Mt Druitt in Western Sydney in 1972. I also began working at the University of Sydney while a student and it was there that I met Aunty Vonnie Gilchrist, my grandmother's cousin, whose parents raised my grandmother and her siblings following the death of their parents. While I had found my father, who was taken at the age of three following his mother's death, I had never met a member of my extended family before. Aunty Vonnie's acceptance and acknowledgement of me and who I am was the start of healing from my trauma of dislocation and abuse. However, the road to reconnection was still bumpy and slow for many reasons.

I completed my degree and went on to study for a PhD, which took many years to complete due to being a single parent and working as well as one of my children having a serious illness. However, despite the temptation to quit many times, I finally reached the end of my studies. As I wrote the final words in my thesis (Green, 2014), I asked the question of how do we decolonise? Then I asked my Ancestors: how do we decolonise; how do I decolonise? They, as sure as there is day and night, answered. The next day, a friend rang and asked me if I had heard of the course at Charles Sturt University in Wiradyuri language and would I do it with her? I had every answer of why I could not do it, I was in my 50th year of life, I had a hearing impairment, and I couldn't cope with English, let alone learning another language. However, I enrolled and completed the Graduate Certificate of Wiradjuri Language, Culture and Heritage and that saw the complete change of direction I had mapped out for the rest of my life. Following my graduation from the course, my daughter enrolled and graduated two years later. My husband has also completed the course and one of my sons is currently doing the course. The course for me was life-changing in so many ways, the most important being the journey of decolonising the structures of my life. Language is culture; culture is language – they cannot be separated because they are one and the same. I was on the journey to coming home to Wiradyuri Country.

Following my daughter's graduation from the course, two years after my own, I received a request to come home and take up the role of Course Director for the Wiradyuri language course at Charles Sturt University. I moved, along with my husband, children and grandchildren, back to Country. While I am still involved in social work, I shifted from teaching social work to teaching within the Wiradyuri language course. I am fortunate to sit with Uncle Stan Grant (Senior) to learn from him and I was fortunate enough to sit with Aunty Flo Grant before she became an ancestor to listen and learn from her about what it is to be Wiradyuri. I am also fortunate enough to work alongside other Wiradyuri people and Wiradyuri allies who are walking the journey of Wiradyuri language restoration and the rebuilding of the Wiradyuri Nation. Together we *ngaabigi winhangagigu* to remember the wisdom of our Ancestors and Wiradyuri *buyaa* (lore/law) and to restore the right way of living on this earth and with each other. We research by examining, trialling and evaluating the information (data) we receive. We sit quietly and ask the Ancestors for advice and guidance. We talk with our Elders and with each other in order to remember and understand what we are being told, hearing and seeing. We read what others have written by interpreting it through our Wiradyuri lens. We look for what is seen and what isn't seen, what is spoken and what isn't spoken. We take all the stories, and we look for the in-between, rather like looking for Dinawan (Emu) in the night sky. You have to look beyond the stars into the milky way and while the stars are part of Dinawan, it is the in-between where Dinawan appears. Much has been said, written and recorded about Wiradyuri people, language and culture but it is the knowledge that Wiradyuri people hold, the knowledge that is in-between the official knowledge, where Wiradyuriness exists, and that is the place where we *ngaabigi winhangagigu*. Wiradyuri are re-searching, re-membering and re-telling Wiradyuri *garigarra* (truth) to heal Country so that all can live well.

Conclusion

An Indigenous nation building methodology, grounded in the Wiradyuri Cosmology, is allowing Wiradyuri people to not only speak their own language again, but to also live a proper Wiradyuri way, that is grounded in Wiradyuri *buyaa*. *Yindyamarra winhanganha* is our aspiration for the past, present and future ways of knowing and understanding our world. As the Wiradyuri Cosmology points out to us, we cannot separate the past from the present or the future, the past is not done and over with but still exists within the present, and the future also exists in the past and the present with the present existing within the past and the future. In the same way that people cannot be separated from their relationships with all else, plants, animals, sky, water and ground, as well as all other people, we also exist within and through those who have come before us and those who will come after us, as they exist through us, and we exist through them.

Indigenous nation building is about Indigenous nations following their own ways of being, doing and knowing, and this is unable to be translated into a western frame. For Wiradyuri people, *ngaabigi winhangaguigu* or, in English, 'research', only exists in its relationship with the researcher and that relationship is the exercise of examining to know and for the purpose of *yindyamarra winhanganha*, respectfully knowing how to live well in a world worth living in. To achieve *yindyamarra winhanganha*, it requires that all people (not just Wiradyuri) who live on Wiradyuri land and everywhere else in the world heal from the sickness that colonisation has created. Wiradyuri people must rebuild their nation and their knowledge systems to that they can practice Wiradyuri *buyaa* once again. People seeking to work with Wiradyuri as allies must be guided by Wiradyuri research methodology which is based on Wiradyuri cultural values and ways of living, comprising *yindyamarra* (respect and honour), *bagaraybang* (to restore, and make comfortable and healthy), *yindyamarra winhanganha* and *muwugamarra* (keep in reserve for future use).

Wiradyuri *ngaabigi winhangaguigu* in order to know and live by the wisdom of our Ancestors and to return to proper ways once again.

Note

[1] Wiradyuri is spelt two different ways in this chapter – Wiradyuri is the Wiradyuri spelling and then Wiradjuri is the English spelling. When speaking about the course title it will be spelt in the English way as per the way it is spelt within the university.

Further reading

Dickson, M. (2020) 'Learning ethics from an echidna: Embedding Indigenous knowledges at the core of ethical research practice', *Methodological Innovations*, 13(3): 1–6.

Hemming, S., Rigney, D., Bignall, S., Berg, S. and Rigney, G. (2019), 'Indigenous nation building for environmental futures: Murrundi flows through Ngarrindjeri country', *Australasian Journal of Environmental Management*, 26(3): 216–235.

Reid, T. (2020) '2020: The year of reckoning, not reconciliation', *Griffith Review 67 Matters of Trust*. Available from: https://www.griffithreview.com/articles/2020-year-of-reckoning/ [Accessed 24 June 2023].

Rigney, D., Bignall, S., Vivian, A. and Hemming S. (2022) 'Indigenous nation building and the political determinants of health and wellbeing', *Discussion Paper*, Melbourne: Lowitja Institute.

References

Charles Sturt University (2023a) Graduate Certificate in Wiradjuri Language, Culture and Heritage. Available from: https://study.csu.edu.au/courses/graduate-certificate-wiradjuri-language-culture-heritage [Accessed 17 October 2023].

Charles Sturt University (2023b) *Our Ethos*. Available from: https://about.csu.edu.au/our-university/ethos [Accessed 24 June 2023].

Gapps, S. (2021) *Gudyarra. The First Wiradyuri War of Resistance. The Bathurst War, 1822–1824*, Sydney: NewSouth Publishing.

Grant, S. (2022) *Conversation*, 15 March 2022.

Grant, S. and Rudder, J. (2010) *A New Wiradjuri Dictionary*, Wagga Wagga: Restoration House Publications.

Grant, S. and Rudder, J. (2014) *A Grammar of Wiradjuri Language*, Wagga Wagga: Restoration House Publications.

Grant, S., Grant, F., Warren, S., Tye, L., Woods, R., Evans, D. and Harris, L. (2015) *Yindyamarra Yambuwan* [Vimeo], directed by Bernard Sullivan, Wiradyuri Country: Charles Sturt University. Available from: https://vimeo.com/140548913 [Accessed 4 June 2023].

Green, S. (2014) 'The history of Aboriginal welfare in the colony of New South Wales 1788–1856', PhD thesis, Kensington, University of New South Wales.

Green, S., Evans, D. and Harris, L. (2020) *Wiradyuriness: IKC301 Wiradjuri Language Lecture, April Intensive*, Wagga Wagga: Charles Sturt University.

University of Arizona (2022) 'What is January in Tucson?', *Indigenous Governance Program*. Available from: https://igp.arizona.edu/jit [Accessed 17 August 2022].

Vivian, A., Jorgensen, M., Cornell, S., Rigney, D., Hemming, S. and Bell, D. (2017) 'Enlivening Indigenous methodologies in Indigenous public policy research', *Ngiya: Talk the Law*, 5: 47–74.

Towards a scholarship of Critical Lived Experience Engagement: big feelings, big stories, big learning

Rebecca J. Moran

Key points

- This chapter disrupts the academy by proposing an ethical framework to engage with lived experience, namely Critical Lived Experience Engagement.
- Learning about lived experience work from the perspective of a lived experience expert requires engaging in complex questions about how lived experience is used, commodified and utilised.
- Lived experience expertise can be used in transformative education, by critically engaging with the elements a lived experience expert uses to achieve such transformations.
- Trauma-informed practice must be modelled and embodied in training on this topic.
- Critical Lived Experience Engagement is one of the most powerful and effective methods to drive policy and practice change across social services.

Introduction

Like all of us, I am many things. I am a wife and mother, a gardener, a poet, a sculptor, singer and songwriter, a research academic – and a 'lived experience expert'. 'Lived experience' is a frequently heard phrase now, generally referring to the expertise a person carries due to their personal experience of something: for example, a mental health 'lived experience expert' will have a personal history of experiencing mental distress. When I started working as a lived experience expert, I did not know a name for this work, or that other people were doing it too. I began as an invited (unpaid) guest speaker to assist in the training of specialist 'rape first response' police officers in the United Kingdom. For the first time, I spoke to a group of strangers, telling them parts of my vulnerable, private, sacred stories, in the hope that this would help create a system that treated people better than how I had been treated in a similar system. I didn't think very much about what I would say or how the audience might receive or experience my stories. I was dissociated, hypervigilant, experiencing trauma intrusions, overwhelmed, deeply distressed, and standing alone with no guidance or support.

Nonetheless, I saw something happen to the officers at the training session as I told my story and revealed the perspective of a sexual violence victim ensnared in a police investigation and public prosecution. Some cried, some asked questions, but all were clearly captivated by what I had to say. This was new to me: I had been a homeless, drug-addicted teenager, and had spent much of my early 20s in the public mental health system in Australia. I had been placed on a permanent disability pension when I turned 18, transitioning from Youth Allowance straight to government disability benefits, with multiple mental health diagnoses and an apparently grim prognosis. Much as I needed that money, I am still saddened that I was examined and classified at 18 as someone who was irreparably damaged, who would never be able to work. While I wasn't paid for this guest appearance at the police academy, for the first time I felt like, maybe, I did have something useful to offer. Maybe the very experiences that had 'disabled' me could be turned into something useful, meaningful and important.

The therapeutic or cathartic potential of lived experience work is enormous, but not without risks and problems, and can feel wildly out of control at times. I almost jumped in front of a train after my first lived experience gig. I was dissociated, distressed, deeply triggered, had not yet been able to do much of my life's trauma processing work, and did not have any opportunity to debrief with or seek support from anyone. This was the first time I had spoken my story aloud outside of fragments in hospital admissions and in therapists' offices, and it gushed out of me without purposefulness or containment. I talked and cried for over three hours, and then walked dazedly out of the police academy alone. This was in 2009, and the organisation that had invited me to speak did not have an established framework for lived experience engagement, so there was no support available to me at the time.

Work led to work, and I was gradually able to put a few things on my CV, which was otherwise full of fruit-picking and labouring jobs. I got better at tailoring content for specific topics and specific audiences, and occasionally got paid for my work. I learned not to pour my whole self out, and thus became slightly less emptied and re-traumatised by each new piece of lived experience work. I benefited psychologically, financially and socially from this new work: it helped me to learn that I had agency and power in this world, and in many ways, this experience has combated toxic shame and experiences of powerlessness associated with complex trauma. There were, however, still times where shame and trauma were deepened through my experiences of doing lived experience work in less-than-ideal conditions.

I was lucky to find two other lived experience educators/experts and teamed up with Rufus May and Eleanor Longden. Together, we wrote one- and two-day training packages, delivered guest lectures at universities and ran a large weekly group meeting where people with lived experience came to speak and be heard, and to listen. I learned more about the long political history of the consumer movement and lived experience campaigning, and became aware that, as lived experience Elder Lyn Mahboub always reminds me, I was "standing on the shoulders of giants". While I had started out in this work alone, I came to understand that there was a strong lived experience community of activists, educators, peer workers, consultants and advisors, and that this movement had been active for decades, paving the way for new generations of lived experience workers like me. Over what is now more than 15 years of training, education and advisory work, specialising in the area of complex trauma and drawing on lived, professional and practice expertise, I have witnessed what I believe to be the unrivalled potential for transformative learning when lived experience is safely and purposefully brought into the room (see also Moran et al, 2022).

There came a time when the cathartic and meaning-making benefits of lived experience were no longer as present or relevant for me, but I continue to campaign for and participate in lived experience engagement. I remain a firm believer that it is not only politically and ethically crucial that lived experience expertise is recognised and valued, but also that lived experience engagement is one of the most powerful and effective methods to drive policy and practice change across social services. This is not limited to the field of mental health: a prime example is the world-leading Australian Government Royal Commission into Institutional Responses to Child Sexual Abuse (McClellan et al, 2017), which engaged with over 8,000 people with lived experience of child sexual abuse and has led to significant change in public awareness and understanding of the issues, as well as driving an array of policy and practice changes. The Royal Commission was impressive in its dignifying engagement with lived experience, but processes for inviting lived experience participation were developed as the Commission proceeded, and were not always ideal (Moran and Salter, 2022). Beyond a common commitment to frameworks such as trauma-informed practice and co-production, many engagements with lived experience are being worked out 'on the fly', leaving space for poor practice that may be ineffective, or even harmful.

Lived experience: power and problems

'Lived experience' (or perhaps more accurately, *living* experience) is a phrase we hear more and more often in community services, at all levels of government, and in academic scholarship, along with words such as co-design and co-production. I wonder, though, how many people are confident in their understanding of what these mean and how they might be embodied, and how many feel a vague sense of guilty confusion because these terms still feel slippery and difficult to understand. I'll admit: I've worked as a 'lived experience expert' for many years and still sometimes feel the guilty confusion.

Lived experience is now used in several ways, including the inclusion of lived experience voices in advisory groups and via consultancy, in tertiary education (curricula content and marking students' work), in non-government organisations, community organisations and publicly funded services (sometimes through the employment of peer workers). The state of Victoria is the first in Australia to form a Lived Experience Directorate within the Department of Health, staffed with lived experience experts (Department of Health, 2022). The word is spreading quickly now, that inclusion of lived experience expertise is becoming part of expected design and ethical delivery standards. This is in no small part due to the activism and advocacy of lived experience experts for close to 50 years. As someone who has been part of that campaign for many years, I feel a mixture of relief, exuberance and concern that we seem finally to be heard. I am excited that change is happening fast, but I believe there is reason for concern and will unpack some of the issues I worry about here.

There are more and more people with lived experience being approached, invited and listened to in community services and academia, but ultimately, most people and services are figuring it out as they go, without a great deal of guidance or support. This can lead to interactions with lived experience experts that are unintentionally invalidating, patronising and in conflict with one of the core ethical principles for working with lived experience: upsetting the imbalance of power between 'the service user' and every other kind of expert (see, for example, Clover, 2011; Foster, 2016; Gustafson et al, 2019). An example of this would be inviting a lived experience guest speaker but paying them at a lower rate than any other consultant. This does not challenge the status quo of power distribution, nor does it challenge the 'othering' of lived experience experts. It is not collaborative or empowering.

In the Australian context, the National Lived Experience (Peer) Workforce Development Guidelines [National Guidelines] (National Mental Health Commission, 2022) state that 'A thriving mental health Lived Experience [Peer] Workforce is a vital component of quality, recovery-focused mental health services', and offer a set of principles for engaging with lived experience workers. Such principles inform the mental health plans and policies guiding the country's mental health care services (employment of peer workers, for example) but do not extend to the many other ways in which lived experience is being utilised. It is not just mental health services who are (or should be) seeking to engage with lived experience, but most other fields of practice do not have any guidelines to offer direction or support.

Even these National Guidelines do not provide a definition of what 'lived experience' is. There is a vague, generalised understanding that 'lived experience' refers to people who have experiences of accessing services or caring for someone who has accessed services. But what about lived experience of domestic and family violence, of imprisonment or detention, of racism, discrimination and injustice? And what kinds of views within that lived experience do community services, government and academia wish to hear and integrate into their practices?

I argue that it is generally a white, tidy, not-too-confronting person with lived experience, someone from the 'Goldilocks zone' of lived experience, who is selected (Moran et al, 2022). This is the kind of lived experience that is easily commodified, easily consumed and not too challenging to interact with. 'Messier' examples of lived experience are rarely accessed in lived experience work, potentially presenting a skewed view of the issue that does not adequately consider intersectional disadvantage and multiple marginalisation.

Further, within the community of lived experience experts, there can be disagreement around what it is that this workforce should be doing. There are also some vast differences in political or critical social positioning. For example, one person with lived experience may describe experiencing relief and benefits from receiving a diagnosis, while another may describe iatrogenic (that is, induced) harm from medication, and consider their treatment in institutions or by services as violating their human rights, enacting a significant power imbalance, and undermining one's dignity.

Which lived experience expert is 'right' about this? Personally, I argue that lived experience must be a fundamentally critical discipline, interrogating power imbalances, discrimination and injustice – but who am I to silence the voice of someone with a different lived experience perspective to mine?

I also have misgivings about the way lived experience can be used as an unchallengeable authority, something that I would argue is problematic in any discipline. Currently, to question a point from someone who speaks from a lived experience perspective is likely to be considered as invalidating that person's experience – and it may well be. As someone who has been doing this work for many years, I welcome questions and critical engagement, though I very rarely get them. I explicitly state to students, audiences, advisory groups, or whoever I may be working with, that I am comfortable to be questioned on any point. This was not the case when I started using my lived experience voice though: back then, I was fragile, prone to shame in the aftermath of speaking publicly about my experiences, and prone to suicidality as a response to shame. I was also alone, unpaid, untrained and largely unsupported by organisations who engaged my services.

This experience of being alone, unpaid, untrained and largely unsupported is still common. Such situations sit in conflict with the core issues engagement with lived experience are intended to address, that is, valuing and amplifying lived experience perspectives and knowledge. But despite these complexities and questions, I am still a believer in the power of the lived experience voice, and in the power of story. I have seen hundreds, maybe thousands, of people experience transformational learning facilitated by incorporating lived experience in education and training. I have seen the richness that can come from working skilfully with lived experience advisory groups – but also the problems that occur when an institution seeks to include lived experience engagement but does not have a clear sense of how this should be done ethically and effectively.

For example, I have been asked to perform tasks that far exceed the scope in proportion to the amount paid, and I have seen tokenistic inclusion of lived experience in policy. The fight for recognition and respect is not over yet; lived experience engagement to date has not balanced the epistemic injustices that so many people with experience of mental distress, trauma, discrimination, marginalisation and intersectional disadvantage can face.

I have seen unexpected problems with lived experience engagement, for example, competitive and unsupportive dynamics around opportunities for lived experience work. Another example is the potential for unhelpful and inaccurate ideas of homogeneity of lived experience, or the generalisation of one lived experience perspective to ecosystems or circumstances where it does not fit. There is so much to explore and learn around lived experience engagement, and now is the time to do it.

Passing for human

In this section, I offer a personal vignette that I have shared as an educator drawing on lived, academic and practice experience. I then unpack what can be learned or reconsidered in response to this 'story'. While I use the example of an education or training setting, the same issues and principles can apply to other lived experience engagement roles, such as advisory group member or lived experience consultant.

'I am in my very early twenties, wearing multiple layers of black "court" clothing – as formal and normal as I can manage with my disability pension budget and the fears I soothe by wearing strange layers of clothes. Long skirt over long pants, long-sleeved t-shirts over singlets, long, loose cardigans over everything, even in the summer. I am compelled to dress this way: a child part of me has theorised that if I put enough layers of clothes on, abusers won't be able to get to my body. This has never stopped anyone, but I can't leave the house if I don't do it.

My body is a source of annihilating shame. I try to breathe quietly, because even this essential bodily action is repulsive – only for me: other people deserve to breathe, are allowed to breathe. I have a noticeable tremor in my hands, I'm grinding my teeth. I am terrified. I carry conflicting beliefs that I made it all up and that it happened. I have a deep knowledge that I am a monster, that I am not human, and that every day I get away with passing for human creates a cosmic imbalance that I have to correct with self-harm and starvation.

Under my long black sleeves are multiple self-harm injuries, some fresher than others. At the courthouse, I am standing with my detective, Colin, sticking to him like a life buoy. This is the final day of the Crown Prosecution's case against one of the men who had sexually assaulted and abused me when I was a kid. I have already "won" one trial against a different offender, with the perp sentenced to eight and a half years in prison. Giving evidence and being questioned by the defence (from a CCTV room in a different part of the building) had been stunningly hard, but I'd done it, and we won despite me being a junkie scum psych patient witness.

After sentencing, I tried to kill myself for being such a monster, for ruining this poor man's life. This was one of several suicide attempts through the three years it took to get from reporting to the police to sentencing on the two cases. Each time, I was outraged to wake up in ICU [Intensive Care Unit], not dead, again. I would transfer from ICU to a psych bed and spend the next few weeks convincing staff that if they let me out, I wouldn't do it again. For a few months, they would limit the amount of medication I could collect in one go, and eventually this would be relaxed too. I'd immediately start siphoning off meds into my "just in case" stash. Just in case I need to kill myself.

My detective, Colin, is a safe place. When he moves, I move, so that I am always right by his side. He believes me. He makes my whole future possible. He is baffling and life-saving – he seems to really think I'm a person, that I am telling the truth, and that the things that have happened aren't my fault. It seems like he has no trouble at all with the question of who is to blame, or confusion about who the monster is. Over the years, I have called him repeatedly to tell him it's me, the monster is me. I made it all up. I'm an attention-seeker, like everybody says. I'm so sick and wrong that I let a man go to jail for something that didn't happen/wasn't that bad/maybe I misunderstood/no-one else would complain about/I made him do it/the knife wasn't really meant as a threat/it's my breasts, it's just because I have big breasts. Like the perp said at the time, and like so many others had said too: *look what you're making me do.*

It's me. The monster is me.

Colin and I wait, not talking much. We've been told that there is a shortage of Crown Prosecutors, and so my case (which is actually the perp's case – I am just a witness for the Crown) has been passed out to a pair of private barristers, whom I have never met, and who know nothing more of my story than the briefs of evidence they have just received. The double doors of the corridor swing open, and I know it is them. They are clean people. Clean, not dirty or sick like me. They wear beautiful suits and carry an armload of important folders. They are talking to each other and laughing – until they turn and see their witness. Me. Their smiles drop from their faces. They are appalled. This is going to ruin their day. They don't think they can win with a witness like me. Their distaste and disappointment are clear on their faces and in their voices when they speak to me. I am even more terrified, even more ashamed.

The barristers do not want to go to trial. They are concerned I will not make a good witness, that I am too unstable. They ask us to wait while they go speak to the defence, to see if they can arrange a last-minute guilty plea to lesser charges to avoid me appearing in court. I feel like I have failed. I was right: I am the monster, the mess, the strange one, the dirty one, the one that has never touched a suit as expensive as the ones they wear.

The defence take the deal. I'm not someone who can stand in a courtroom and credibly repeat what my police statement swears to. The man who raped me dozens of times pleads guilty to a few counts of indecent dealings with a child and receives an 18-month suspended sentence. I crumple and fall in the lift on the way out of the building and spend the next three weeks in hospital being treated for liver failure. I hadn't noticed until then that I was yellow with jaundice, or how much my abdomen hurt.

For years, I had lived from court date to court date, disintegrating every time they arraigned or postponed a date my heart had been racing to for months. I know I am one of the lucky ones: my reports led to two convicted perpetrators. I had a brilliant detective who made me the person I am today: with his unbudgeable belief, and his simple assumption that I was a person – maybe even a *good* person.

Seventeen years later, I still feel gutted like a fish when I picture the barristers' faces the moment they saw how hopeless their witness was. I am sure they were working to protect me as well as their own reputations, but I am still annihilated by shame when I see the micro-expressions of disgust in their eyes and around the corners of their mouths. I am not clean enough, sane enough, credible enough. I was right about how disgusting I am. I am put in my place by their suits, their judgement, and their power. I am the hysteric, the attention-seeker, the Other.'

Learning from stories

I have used this story to teach trauma-informed practice in professional development settings, and in university teaching in areas such as social work. There are many things I want students to learn from this story, and I think that they learn these lessons primarily through their emotional responses – through their big feelings. Students have cried openly while I've told this story; others have expressed their anger towards the barristers or picked up my love for the detective who walked so steadily beside me.

Students who encounter this story are in some way in a relationship with me. The very first thing I do with any roomful of trainees, students, or any other group I am working with, is to build a strong, positive relationship with everybody present. I do this the moment people start coming into the room: when setting up tea, coffee or technology, when telling people where the toilets are, when unstacking chairs. Essentially, I need to get them to like, respect and trust me. I use humour, warmth, friendliness and a subtle tone of confidence and authority that tells participants, "You are in capable, aware, and caring hands."

A sense of humour is very valuable to build connection and put people at ease. It is also useful for providing relief from tension in challenging moments of learning. I 'read the room' to ascertain the type and tone of humour I can use with each group and let this evolve throughout the period of contact. I think about details, including the way I dress (should I cover self-harm scars?) and the way I set up a room. I pay attention to the comfort needs of students, and always begin with exercises to co-produce safety in the room.

I work to build connection, trust and even affection in these relationships. This is mutual: I endeavour to see the best in any person or group I work with, and aim to create spaces where students can thrive, as well as being able to make mistakes, do clumsy practice runs, and explore their own experiences and emotions safely. When students hear this story, I believe that most of them have come to care about me, so any empathy and compassion they might feel in listening to this story is attached to a real person. I believe this personal connection deepens the learning: this isn't just a sad story, it's a sad story about someone they know and potentially care for, trust, relate to, admire or like.

I want students to understand the pervasive and devastating shame that complex and compounded trauma causes. I try to describe that shame – a shame so deep that I don't even feel human – in ways that students will be able to understand, but not be crushed by. This is another reason I use humour in my lived experience teaching, and why I work so extensively to create a safe space and model emotional safety for students. I need them to come with me to extreme places: places where big feelings are intentionally activated. Over many years of this work, I have learned how to sail that ship safely and surely enough to be able to go close to the edge of the world without students falling off into the void. Trauma-informed practice must be modelled and embodied in training on this topic, and the emotional safety of students taken seriously while allowing space for development, growth and big learning.

I want students to think deeply about 'positioning' when they hear this story. I want them to understand the many ways I was positioned as the tainted, hopeless Other. I believe discussion of micro-expressions to be important, and I want to convey how devastating it can be to feel and show disgust towards a person. I tell students that this isn't about learning to control their faces. It is about learning to see and love the innate worth and hope that is everybody's birthright. I tell students that they will likely need to hold this hope and love for people in times when the person cannot see or hold it for themselves. This is not something that can be faked, especially if one is working with young people or trauma survivors, whose instincts are sharpened, and who are likely to be deeply affected by micro-expressions of 'othering' responses such as disgust. As my story tells, I already felt worthless, disgusting and sub-human before I saw disgust on the barristers' faces.

Healing trauma requires experiences counter to those present in the dynamics of abuse and trauma: for example, shame and self-disgust must be countered with experiences of compassion, positive regard and dignity. I ask students to reflect on how the way they present and position themselves can shift others into positions of otherness, disempowerment and shame, or alternatively, into positions of empowerment, dignity and agency. I ask students to identify the factors in this vignette that relate to power and position, and to critically reflect on how similar factors might play out in their own practice.

I also present this vignette, along with others, to prompt continuing self-reflection on students' own biases and any stigmatising beliefs or attitudes they might be carrying. I intentionally confront them with the fact that the professionally dressed, competent and powerful person telling them this story was once a junkie they might avoid sitting next to on the train, the homeless kid they don't know how to look at, the uncontained, emotional psychiatric patient covered in self-inflicted wounds. I emphasise the importance of believing people and explain epistemic injustice.

Here, too, the quality of relationship I have worked to build with students is important, as is the necessity to avoid shaming or blaming students for the less-than-ideal treatment I have received in systems and services. I aim to strike a careful balance, one which evokes a sense of passion, commitment and an ethical obligation, but which does not leave students feeling hopeless, overwhelmed or othered themselves. I work to include solutions as well as pointing out problems, and I present these solutions in such a way that I hope they feel achievable and within reach. In this way, I hope that students will go on to be champions of change, and that, gradually, our systems and services will improve.

Building a discipline: Critical Lived Experience Engagement

I would like to see lived experience engagement develop into a vigorous, lively, critical discipline, and this cannot happen if it is didactic, segregated, homogenised and sanitised. While I wish to deeply validate the views and experiences of lived experience experts who promote the medical model, I am unsure whether this contributes to what I will call for now Critical Lived Experience Engagement scholarship. The medical model is already well-represented across disciplines, and I see critical engagement with traditional, patriarchal, disempowering, colonising systems to be a key focus for lived experience engagement. I consider Critical Lived Experience Engagement scholarship as compatible with intersectional feminism, as well as being relevant in areas of scholarship such as human rights studies, decolonial studies, social work, sociology and criminology.

To develop into a rigorous discipline, Critical Lived Experience Engagement must include space for asking questions and exploring differing views; the capacity for critical dialogue is essential. A didactic, 'walking on eggshells' approach to lived experience engagement does not always leave or create a fertile, open space for vigorous discussion, introducing different ideas, or questioning the views and guidance lived experience experts offer. I am, of course, not suggesting that the validation of and respect for lived experience experts' stories and experiences is not important: it is an essential and important part of the socio-political change and recognition that the consumer movement has spent decades fighting for.

Doing lived experience work should be safe, and experts should not be exposed to unacceptable risks of invalidation and re-traumatisation. I say 'unacceptable' risk because lived experience work effectively means signing up for an activity with inherent risk of encountering triggers and potentially re-traumatisation. Lived experience experts are also exposed to reputational impacts, exposure to stigma and discrimination, and even more serious risks such as unwanted mental health or child protection interventions. These risks can be particularly heightened if grief and trauma are still very raw, or in lived experience engagement with difficult groups, for example, compulsory professional development training.

Many universities now have a lived experience research unit (for example, the Australian National University's Lived Experience Research Unit, Curtin University's Valuing Lived Experience Project, and the University of Melbourne's ALIVE Centre), with some integrating lived experience engagement into teaching too. Academics may have to relinquish control and face challenges to their familiar, traditional ways of doing research. Lived experience engagement is birthing new methodologies that need to be worked through with ethics and integrity – and, I would argue, engagement with trauma-informed and decolonising frameworks.

The ALIVE National Centre for Mental Health Research Translation (2022) is one institute engaging with this issue and seeking to develop robust frameworks for integrating lived experience as evidence in applied mental health research. This includes the birthing of new methodologies, as well as re-casting roles within research teams. There is growing promotion of the idea that lived experience is a valid type of evidence – an idea in conflict with many of the entrenched traditions of scientific research, particularly in the natural sciences.

Social science research that engages with lived experience, such as this edited book, remains open to criticism that this approach is not a rigorous, replicable and therefore credible form of evidence, but this is changing rapidly. Many questions remain unexplored in this area and in the domain of research ethics: for example, is lived experience engagement intended to serve as a cathartic and meaningful part of lived experience experts' recovery journeys, or is it about improving research processes and outcomes? For many researchers engaging with lived experience, these are grey areas that we are just beginning to discuss and examine.

Lived experience engagement is emerging as a distinct scholarship, which means that this is a perfect time to strengthen the critical aspects of the discipline using a Critical Lived Experience Engagement lens. It is my hope that delineations between lived experience expert and non-lived experience researchers fade, promoting equality and reducing the risk of discrimination or discrediting such experts. Researchers in this area could be supported in communities of practice with ongoing and deeper conversations in the literature.

The cathartic and social mobility potential of lived experience engagement work is not to be discounted, but we must continue to work out ways to protect dignity and equity, as well as considering safety and credibility issues. As my autobiographical introduction demonstrates, doing lived experience engagement work can help people previously excluded from the workforce because of their experiences to find a pathway to employment, education and training opportunities, and in my case, eventual social class mobility. However, I would not advise anyone to follow my early pathway, when I was unsupported and unsafe, with no framework or community to guide me in my lived experience work.

I can now use my own lived experience work as a launching pad to identify what might be some of the useful components of a lived experience engagement protocol or practice framework. With regard to wellbeing and access to appropriate benefits, one obvious issue is that I should have been paid consultant fees for my time. Another problem is that I should have been supported before, during and after my participation, and had debriefing planned into the lived experience engagement process. More subtle issues include the benefits of training and preparation prior to commencing lived experience work, both in the reflective practice of experts and in organisational processes. For example, this could include preparatory meetings to discuss the purpose and scope of the lived experience engagement. Lived experience experts could be supported and encouraged to explore their reasons for wanting to do this work, to reflect on any risks and benefits, and consider which parts of their experiences they wish to share and why. Co-produced safety plans could be built into lived experience engagement, along with a focus on informed consent, in the hope that this might reduce future shame or regret for lived experience experts.

Conclusion

This chapter is just a preliminary, and largely personal, exploration of some of the complexities of lived experience engagement in its current form. I have raised a number of issues without providing answers or solutions to all these tensions. I cannot do this as a single lived experience expert, and I do not suggest that my experience can be generalised. It is my hope that we will see purposeful and reflexive lived experience engagement across many sectors, and that those involved will have a wealth of shared knowledge to draw on.

This is an exciting time: the birth of a new discipline. In saying this, I am not dismissing the rich work that has been done around lived experience for decades. Rather, I am calling for further development of a strong and purposeful critical scholarship that will enrich lived experience engagement, support safety, fairness and equity, and develop innovative and powerful methodologies to address social and epistemic injustices and improve systems and services, while simultaneously providing dignifying and healing experiences for those involved.

Acknowledgements
It is important that I acknowledge not only the many members of the social movement that has brought us to where we are today, but also the people in my life that I have spent years discussing these issues with. Many people have contributed to how I think about lived experience engagement, but I must make special mention of Dr Robyn Martin, Lyn Mahboub, Craig Hughes-Cashmore (and the rest of the gang), Aimee Sinclair, Dr Sophie Ridley, Debbie Cleland and Josh Moorhouse. Thank you, deep thinkers.

Further reading

Moran, R.J. and Asquith, N.L. (2020) 'Understanding the vicarious trauma and emotional labour of criminological research', *Methodological Innovations*, 13(2): 1–11.

Moran, R.J. and Ridley, S. (2021) 'Trauma informed and dignifying practice in qualitative research', *New Voices in Social Work Research*. Available from: https://newvoicesinsocialworkresearch.wordpress.com/ [Accessed 4 December 2022].

Pratt, B. (2021) 'Achieving *inclusive* research priority-setting: What do people with lived experience and the public think is essential?', *BMC Medical Ethics*, 22(117): 1–14.

Roennfieldt, H. and Byrne, L. (2020) ' "How much 'lived experience' is enough?" Understanding mental health lived experience work from a management perspective', *Australian Health Review*, 44(6): 898–903.

References

ALIVE National Centre for Mental Health Research Translation (2022) *Transforming Mental Health and Well-being through Primary Care and Community Action*. Available from: https://alivenetwork.com.au/ [Accessed 11 December 2022].

Clover, D. (2011) 'Successes and challenges of feminist arts-based participatory methodologies with homeless/street-involved women in Victoria', *Action Research*, 9(1): 12–26.

Department of Health (2022) *Lived Experience*. Available from: https://www.health.vic.gov.au/mental-health-reform/lived-experience [Accessed 11 December 2022].

Foster, V. (2016) *Collaborative Arts-based Research for Social Justice*, Oxon: Routledge.

Gustafson, D.L., Parsons, J.E. and Gillingham, B. (2019) 'Writing to transgress: Knowledge production in Feminist Participatory Action Research', *Forum: Qualitative Social Research*, 20(2): Article 17.

McClellan, P., Atkinson, B., Coate, J., Fitzgerald, R., Milroy, H. and Murray, A (2017) *Royal Commission into Institutional Responses to Child Sexual Abuse: Final Report*. Commonwealth of Australia. Available from: https://www.childabuseroyalcommission.gov.au/final-report [Accessed 4 June 2023].

Moran, R. and Salter, M. (2022) 'Therapeutic politics and the institutionalisation of dignity: "Treated like the Queen"', *The Sociological Review*, 70(5): 969–985.

Moran, R.J., Martin, R. and Ridley, S. (2022) ' "It helped me open my eyes": Incorporating lived experience perspectives in social work education', *Affilia*, 1–16.

National Mental Health Commission (2022) *National Lived Experience (Peer) Workforce Development Guidelines*. Available from: https://www.mentalh ealthcommission.gov.au/lived-experience/lived-experience-workforces/ peer-experience-workforce-guidelines/national-lived-experience-(peer)- workforce-develop [Accessed 11 December 2022].

PART II

Scrutinising lived experience research processes through leadership and collaboration

4

Lived experience perspectives on a co-design process: the 'Under the Radar' men's suicide prevention project

3

Stephen Lake, Anonymous Lived Experience Advisors, Campbell Clerke, William Crompton, Norman Stevens, Ivan Ma, John O'Loughlin, Peter Sutton and Matt Whitten

Key points

- This chapter disrupts the academy by explaining how the experiences of people with lived experience of suicidal ideation should be considered and addressed in collaborative research on this topic.
- People with lived experience must have agency and equality with project team members throughout the research and co-design processes, with the same people with lived experience involved throughout.
- We should be encouraged to share our experiences to challenge traditional research-based and practice paradigms that often fail to legitimise subjective experience and experiential insight.
- Suicide should not be viewed as a disease in search of a cure. Given the life experiences and circumstances of individuals with suicidal ideation, it can seem to be a perfectly rational choice, and their reality must be validated and respected as 'normal' before help is offered.

Introduction

Suicide is the leading cause of death for Australians aged 15 to 44 years (Australian Bureau of Statistics, 2020). Between 50 and 60 per cent of individuals who die by suicide 'fly under the radar', that is, without receiving formal mental health care (Johnston et al, 2009). Most have been in contact with services for physical health issues in the days or months preceding an attempt but did not receive help for their suicidal thoughts or mental health problems (Stene-Larsen and Reneflot, 2019). Little is known about individuals at risk of suicide who are not receiving mental health care.

In 2021, the Black Dog Institute, a mental health research organisation in Sydney, Australia, undertook a four-year research project to develop a person-centred service for individuals at risk of suicide but not in care. The project consisted of multiple phases and several stakeholders including a project manager, institute research teams, a design team, a lived experience team and representatives from external organisations. The project aimed to adhere to a co-design methodology and a governance structure was created with a Core Co-Design team established at the outset. At the time of writing this chapter (August 2022), the first three phases had been completed.

Phase 1 involved two systematic reviews of existing literature regarding people who died by suicide but were not in receipt of services. Key risk factors identified for being 'under the radar' were: male sex, both younger and older age, rural location, and the absence of a mental health diagnosis (Tang et al, 2022). A lack of Australian data was identified. Phase 2 aimed to understand suicide-related lived experience among Australian men in particular. This was achieved via a survey with 450 respondents, and 49 in-depth qualitative interviews led by two research teams. Phase 3 aimed to design a model of care to meet the needs of the target population with a stakeholder group, including men recruited specifically as Lived Experience Advisors in this phase. Three Lived Experience Advisors were involved in the initial planning of this project, but they were not the same advisors who were involved in Phase 3. At the time of writing, the proposed intervention and its trial were still being finalised.

This chapter focuses on Phase 3, from the perspectives of the Lived Experience Advisors.

The process

A design team led Phase 3, which focused more on human-centred design than co-design principles. Sixteen men with lived experience, most aged in their 50s and 60s, many of whom were interviewed in Phase 2, were invited to participate in developing a support service or intervention that would be appealing to men defined as 'under the radar', through a series of workshops. Eleven of those men have co-authored this chapter. The men were divided into two groups: a 'design team' alongside various professionals and academics to develop an intervention for men 'under the radar'; and a 'test team' comprised only of men with lived experience to provide feedback on those ideas. The design team consisted of 25 academics and other professionals, not identified by their professional role or lived experience, but collectively labelled 'designers'.

The number of workshops originally planned was greater than those that were eventually held, due to COVID-19 pandemic constraints and the need to conduct workshops online, limiting the participation of the men in both teams.

The Lived Experience Advisors identified several issues from Phase 3, including:

- Lack of clarification of 'rules of engagement' for interactions with Lived Experience Advisors, which led to the design team often failing to recognise the significance of cues they gave.
- The practice of assigning people the role of a 'designer' during the design workshops that prohibited participants with clinical training or lived experience from sharing their expertise.
- Informing the Lived Experience Advisors that preparatory research had been conducted, but not presenting the findings to them.
- Lack of information about project constraints from the outset, which limited the scope of proposed interventions, so that many ideas were considered that could not be developed. This lack of information resulted in wasted time and gave rise to false hopes.
- Intense time pressure in the final workshop.
- Seemingly greater importance ascribed to 'the process' than to recognising and addressing issues, and to the outcome.
- A reduced period for collaborative work (due to the COVID-19 pandemic) that limited exploration into existing services to identify how a new intervention would meet a hitherto unmet need.

The precise role and ability of the men to influence the project through the workshops was unclear, and no specific protocols were established to guide and manage any challenges encountered. As the Lived Experience Advisors were recruited only for Phase 3, the need to build trust with them over a very short time was a focus of the Black Dog Institute team. The actual process of Lived Experience Advisors learning to trust strangers in the room, and to find words for things they may not ever have told anybody before, that they had buried deep within themselves and lived with for years and decades alone in crowds, is not something that can easily be squeezed into a few workshop days.

The central mechanism to guide the design process were three 'personas' representing men with different life experiences and ages who could be considered representative of the target group of a proposed intervention. While these personas attempted to integrate previous research findings, many of the Lived Experience Advisors did not recognise themselves in them, despite some of the men being both survey and interview participants in Phase 2. The experiences of the characters did not relate to those of many of the Lived Experience Advisors. This frustrated them, as the project focused on reaching men 'under the radar' with whom they did not identify.

With the project not adapting to prioritise, and not effectively addressing, the needs of such men, the Lived Experience Advisors felt they continued to work with a paradigm that privileged traditional research approaches.

A power divide developed within the design team, as members from the Black Dog Institute were more familiar with the research, although existing findings had not been fully analysed before Phase 3 commenced. Some Lived Experience Advisors were unfamiliar with academic research and felt that team members failed to communicate effectively. These difficulties at times also created a frustrating environment for the men who participated. Better integrating the research into the design phase through another process may have allowed the Lived Experience Advisors to understand how it had influenced the design phase, to identify gaps in knowledge, and to create more realistic personas that resonated with them. An opportunity should have been created for the Lived Experience Advisors to become familiar with the research findings, to critique them in light of their own experiences, and for the outcome of that discussion to then shape the design phase.

The Lived Experience Advisors believe that Phase 3 assumed that men are 'under the radar' because they are unaware of available services, fear stigma attached to seeking help, or because of a conception of masculinity that prevents them from acknowledging that they need help, and therefore sought to address these challenges. However, this narrow understanding of the suicide experiences of men 'under the radar' that informed the design process excluded the fact that some men are 'under the radar' after negative previous contact with mental health professionals. Some Lived Experience Advisors had already sought help, and had clinical diagnoses, but endured harmful experiences with those professionals or found them unable to provide the supports they needed, so that they would not seek further assistance.

Participating men also indicated that they would have liked a more in-depth consideration of the psychological and social experiences leading to suicide, the lifelong effects of abuse and trauma, and individual experiences in the hours preceding an attempted suicide and the patterns attendant upon that time-frame, during which it is highly unlikely either that the individual will seek help in any case or that others might recognise that they are in need of help. These aspects did not appear to have been captured by the literature review.

The Lived Experience Advisors and the Black Dog Institute team discussed these and additional challenges during and immediately after the workshops, when there was ample opportunity to provide feedback and reflect upon the process. The difficulty was primarily that their feedback did not sufficiently inform the process as it continued and had not informed the planning phase.

Some of these identified challenges fell outside the purview of the project as originally planned, but as they were all elements of the Lived Experience Advisors' experience, and potentially that of other men 'under the radar' whom they represented, these still needed to be recognised and addressed by this project as contributions based on lived experience. Addressing these concerns fully would also have improved the potential of a proposed intervention to reach the widest possible target group. In this respect, the workshop process should have been sufficiently flexible and allocated considerably more time to integrate this experiential input. These points illustrate some of the limitations of lived experience involvement and how the process was pre-determined.

The Lived Experience Advisors would have liked the following key issues and experiences to be addressed:

1. The definition of the target group and, hence, the objective of the project, failed to acknowledge the complexity of the lived experience of suicide and the 'under the radar' concept. During the workshops, it quickly became apparent that not everybody in the group had the same understanding of this concept.
2. The need to reform the education, training and practice of psychologists, general practitioners and psychiatrists, as well as the urgent need for substantive improvements to the entire health system was not discussed. Adverse experiences of Lived Experience Advisors and others in the community with these mental health professionals suggest this need for reform.

The Australian public mental health system is reported to be inadequate on multiple levels, including in terms of unaffordability and inaccessibility for many, insufficient crisis resources and a national shortage of psychiatrists (Krasnostein, 2022). Both professionals and others who engage with people at risk, even with the best of intentions, sometimes have the effect of re-traumatising or compounding their problems, rather than helping them. The fact that even government mental health and suicide prevention policies over the past 30 years have not appreciably reduced the incidence of suicide suggests that the 'problem' is not being understood correctly and that the requisite responses are not being invested in. Systemic inadequacies of the national mental health system also include the absence of appropriate regional, rural and remote mental health care; the limited number of psychologists who work within the Medicare system because of the insufficient rebates they are able to access, rendering their services unavailable to many; a chronic shortage of psychiatrists; service providers' refusal to supervise patients with some conditions, meaning that many people cannot access appropriate treatment or diagnoses in their own state and are forced to travel interstate; the years that can pass before a diagnosis is even offered; and the fact that people continue to take their own lives with their conditions not properly recognised.

3. Insufficient education and training of mental health professionals means that how they define the problems they are expected to assist people with are not *adequately* defined at all, and that consequently, they too easily provide inappropriate and unsatisfactory 'care'. This illustrates how knowledge is a contingent social construct, and in this instance, it does not necessarily reflect or take cognisance of international education, research outcomes and practice.

   The fact that some Lived Experience Advisors, as well as the larger population groups whom they represent, have sometimes had prior encounters with mental health professionals also means that, depending upon their backgrounds, they will have some insight into their own problems. They may have informed themselves from a psychological and psychiatric perspective, and they should therefore be permitted to speak to the inadequacies of these perspectives, however threatening that may be to professionals. Many, if not all, of the Lived Experience Advisors in this project had such insights, and the project reflections presented here emerge from that knowledge.

4. There is an over-dependence on prescription medication to manage mental health issues, at the expense of considering other responses (Bell, 2005; Horowitz and Moncrieff, 2022). Medication does not 'cure' anything, nor change life circumstances, which too often people cannot change themselves. Due to side effects of such medication, people can also lose their lives, literally or figuratively. This was the experience of several Lived Experience Advisors.

5. The preliminary research intended to support this project focused on published peer-reviewed studies that examined one or more predictors of non-receipt of formal mental health services among people who died by suicide (Tang et al, 2022). The Lived Experience Advisors felt it would have been helpful to also consider classical studies of suicide (Masaryk, 1881; Durkheim, 1897; Halbwachs, 1930) and more recent studies (for example, Jamison, 1999), published memoirs of people with mental health issues who have attempted suicide (for example, Paperny, 2020), recent research on the lifelong effects of trauma and abuse (for example, Van Der Kolk, 2014; Herman, 2015), and on socio-economic factors influencing suicide (for example, Case and Deaton, 2020).

   The Lived Experience Advisors also believe that it would have been prudent to address the enormous volume of historical, philosophical and multicultural reflections on suicide (for example, Murray, 1998, 2000; Battin, 2015), and other psychological and psychiatric 'schools', all of which they feel would have been useful in informing the design of such a project and improving academic team members' understanding of the challenges they sought to address. Omission of such studies suggests that the scope of the research review was too limited.

6. The premise of many suicide prevention strategies that suicide and mental health conditions leading to it are 'illnesses' that require prevention or cure is not how some of the men felt in this project. This assumption can undermine the need of individuals to have their problems unconditionally understood and accepted, without caveat, that suicide may be a rational choice, and that individuals may wish to end their lives as an autonomous and dignified act, analogous to assisted dying. The Lived Experience Advisors felt strongly that their experiences must first be affirmed, that their outlook is normal for them, however it may appear to others, and that there are valid reasons for them to think and feel as they do. Only when that occurs should we then consider how they can be helped and what form that help should take. It would therefore be appropriate for all working in this field to ask themselves *why* they wish to prevent people from dying by suicide, and what hope of a better life they really have to offer them. Indeed, '[the person attempting] suicide does not reject life as such, but only the terms on which it is being offered to him [*sic*]' (Schopenhauer, 1859: 512).

7. There are several population cohorts with known incidences of suicide, including the Australian Indigenous population, the LGBTQIA+ community, military service personnel, the unemployed, refugees and asylum seekers, victim-survivors of childhood abuse, teenagers, and young adults subject to complex stressors and anxieties imposed upon them by our society and education system and an insecure future, and those with clinical conditions such as schizophrenia and bipolar disorder. Some of the Lived Experience Advisors recruited for the design phase represented several of these groups, but their specific experiences and causes affecting them were not incorporated into the project or envisaged as being addressed by the design outcome, and no discussion of these occurred during the workshop. In this way, too, the ostensible target group was inexplicably limited.

   Another important group of people who were excluded were 'survivors': family and friends of those who had taken their own lives. It is increasingly acknowledged that they also have valuable experience and insights to contribute, which differ from those of the Lived Experience Advisors involved in this project. Indeed, some suicide prevention and support groups have been founded by precisely these 'survivors', and they are also very interested in helping to prevent suicide, but unfortunately, their voice was not heard in this project.

   Instead of considering how being a member of any of these groups directly influenced suicidal ideation, Lived Experience Advisors felt that the attention was on other, arguably less decisive, issues. For example, discussions focused more on ending alcohol and substance abuse than on the reasons *why* such abuse occurred. Similarly, suicide was viewed as a 'problem' without sufficient consideration being given to recognising and addressing its causes. If any decision had been made in the planning phase to limit the target audience by the lack of specific focus on any of these population cohorts and, by extension, many of the causes of suicide, this was not explained to the Lived Experience Advisors.

Perhaps the decisive element across the group of Lived Experience Advisors and these population cohorts is that their sense of self, their integrity as individuals, has been injured, albeit in diverse and often compounding ways. These effects are sometimes intergenerational. Their healing may never be complete and may typically require years of support. This cannot be achieved entirely by mental health professionals, nor by medication or many forms of therapy commonly offered; it requires a whole-of-society, social justice approach. To facilitate this, mental health professionals must embrace a stronger public and political advocacy role, with the focus on social determinants of health. The outcomes of research and projects such as this must be communicated to policy makers and decision-makers in government and the wider community, with the aim of tangibly minimising socio-economic, institutional, employment and other conditions that contribute to mental and physical health problems. Preventing such problems means addressing their origins and causes *before* they become problems; this requires us to create a society in which the likelihood of many people ever becoming suicidal is minimised throughout our lives (Al-Halabí and Fonseca-Pedrero, 2023).

Nonetheless, it is hoped that the intervention emerging from this project will benefit men 'under the radar', while also leading to further improvements and other responses, and that this analysis will lead to better outcomes in other projects. The single greatest benefit of this project was bringing men with lived experience together; they felt understood and unconditionally accepted by each other, and formed a continuing, mutually supportive brotherhood. They acknowledge that they were accepted, and excellently supported by two dedicated Lived Experience team members from the Black Dog Institute, including outside and beyond the workshop phase. This support was crucial to the men's wellbeing, as involvement in such a project can lead to the reliving of trauma. These Lived Experience team members also provided the Lived Experience Advisors with a channel of communication with the remainder of the research team, which the men felt they otherwise did not have. They recognise that the project was well-intentioned. This discussion is not intended to present the Black Dog Institute or individuals in a negative light, and these team members had different insights into how and why these challenges occurred that the Lived Experience Advisors were not always privy to, and which were often beyond team members' control.

The Lived Experience Advisors did not gain a reassuring impression of academic research from this process, and their reservations are reflected throughout this discussion. They inferred from this how researchers appear to be trained in the social sciences today, that our universities no longer educate them in as broad, interdisciplinary and comprehensive a manner as they once did, that they lack much historical and international understanding of their disciplines, and that a variety of other constraints focused on concrete outcomes within limited time-frames also influence funding and processes, so that it is probable that the issues identified here would have occurred in any such project or research institute. Consequently, all of these limitations now play into the unsatisfactory way mental health policies are conceived and implemented on every level.

Key lessons

Four key lessons on co-design can be extrapolated from this discussion:

1. The acknowledgement of multiple roles in the room, the chance for people with diverse perspectives to share knowledge, build trust, and the purposeful elevation of the voices of people with lived experience relevant to the objective of the study, such that outcomes are manifestly informed by their contribution.
2. The importance of having clear communication processes, transparency around decision-making, project scope and constraints from the outset for all groups within a project, and resolution of any power imbalances among participants. One of the central contributions from people with lived experience to suicide prevention research is the added depth of knowledge of the lived experience of suicidal ideation, the ability to test the accuracy of assumptions made by researchers and others about this issue and to diversify the research findings by highlighting experiences not consistent with research conclusions. The design process must allow for an openness to challenge and recognise the breadth and diversity of the suicide experiences of men 'under the radar' and ensure a flexible capacity to continually adapt to issues as they arise throughout such a process.
3. The use of 'personas' in mental health initiatives, especially around service design, should only serve as a guide, rather than the key instrument for developing an intervention.
4. The experiences and perspectives of the men with lived experience in this project demonstrate that if the mental health sector aims to bring the voices of lived experience into initiatives, it is essential to place importance on people over and above processes. Well-established approaches to engaging with a range of stakeholders need not be abandoned. However, the success

of co-design methods hinges on establishing genuine collaboration, specifically around sharing power, building trust, transparency, and open and skilled communication. These conditions fell short within this project, as Phase 3 focused more on the design principles rather than the 'co' of collaboration. This emphasises the inherent challenges of participatory methods and the need for team leaders to acquire a unique skillset to mitigate these challenges and successfully integrate design principles with ethical lived experience engagement. It is critical to hear from the perspective of Lived Experience team members and advisors throughout the process to understand if these criteria are being met. Team members may believe that they are doing this, while Lived Experience Advisors may feel that they aren't, so a continuing mechanism for discussion and feedback that is enabled to *change* the process *during* the project becomes essential. In such participatory projects, people with lived experience need to be invited to join as equal partners, not participants. It could be said that this requires a paradigm shift for the beliefs, attitudes and practices of health professionals. This entails working from a recovery-oriented, strengths-based and trauma-informed approach.

Creative reflections

Lived Experience Advisors felt that their voices were rarely or insufficiently heard and understood during the design phase workshops. They wondered how others expected them to feel and behave and how others tended to view them and their experiences. Their creative works explore these experiences. These are included here, rather than at the beginning of this chapter, because they chronologically follow the actual design phase and result from the men's feelings of disappointment with that process.

Under the radar

Anonymous

To be among men where I require no explanation, where I can connect but not need to speak, to explain, to justify. Where I am not having to second-guess sincerity as others' discomfort requiring me to change. Where my thoughts are not judged, seen as defective or recused from; this lack of hope, this despair, this desire to end as legitimate.

I have been alone, with others who are or have felt deeply the isolation these thoughts bring. Who know the thin line between life and death and do not presume it is not legitimate. Men who will not rescue me but just let me sit, knowing they know and are known.

They say, 'out of the mouth the heart speaks', and though I do not always understand it and though the words may appear wrong, if I listen long enough, not hear it with my ears, I will hear his needs, I will hear the wisdom of his heart.

And in this space, this place we create and now own, any endings are our endings and require our need to grieve. For we have contemplated our own ending, at our own volition, our own timing, with our own hands; to steal the ending from me – the voice I found, the efficacy I felt – feels silenced and weakened and I am left alone again.

Why am I 'under the radar'? Why don't I seek support for my feelings of suicide?

Well 'suicide' is the way you have to describe what I am thinking and feeling. Suicide; a mental health issue that needs treatment, a hopelessness I need rescuing from, a failure of character which can be rebuilt, a failure of vision where 'eyes cast down' can be raised to see the possibility.

I don't seek you out because I do not want to be told my sadness, my wanting to kill myself – Yes, kill myself, not commit suicide – is not valid, reasonable. I don't want what power I feel I have over my world taken from me with a message of incompleteness.

If I speak with you, I need validation, I need you to listen not with your view of the world. Maybe then, once you understand, you may not choose to see me as someone fractured or needing rescuing.

So just sit with me without any preconceived idea so at least my world, for maybe a moment, has two people in it.

My three days at Bronte

J. O'Loughlin

Part of the process in 'Under the Radar' was a three-day planning workshop at Bronte Surf Club in Sydney. Not knowing the actual agenda or format of the workshops at that stage, it was hard to find the courage at first, but starting the journey I decided to approach it with an open mind.

Day one for me was daunting enough but adding the different levels of understanding and language was somewhat more bewildering and given the subject matter, a three-day workshop was nowhere near enough time to tackle the issues that were highlighted, any wonder the first day left me tired and somewhat annoyed that the reasons behind lived experience from the focus group attending were being so undervalued. The twists and turns of the two days that followed only added to my confusion, although the experience did have positive outcomes on a personal level; at least I gained an understanding of the core issues and a direction to follow in my future pursuits, namely, follow up on Peer Work, to have a greater understanding of the shortcomings in the mental health sector and how to make a contribution, however small, towards making a difference.

More than a few months have passed since the workshop, and reflecting back on the experiences has led me to draw several conclusions to make the inclusion of Focus Group Experience Advisors in the planning phase of any future projects more effective, namely:

- Include input from and by Lived Experience Advisors at an earlier stage in the process.
- Keep language simple and jargon-free, as some may not understand and thus the process won't fall over.
- Approach everything with a clear understanding of the common objectives from both sides.
- Be more sympathetic towards the human factor of lived experience: it is all part of how we contribute.

Summarising the experience from the initial survey and phone calls, many Zoom calls and the workshop, has been an experience. If anything, my hope is that more organisations and institutions utilise people who are the focus of research, so that findings or future directions could be more accurate or beneficial.

Dear diary

Anonymous

Remember what it was like when you heard of the project for the first time? I seemingly buried the memory of my past agony deep inside my heart. Today marks the end of our workshops, yet it is hardly the end to combating the ever-lurking shadow. Gathered from different walks of life, we proposed, designed and refined a programme devoted to seeking those who have yet to be found. It has never been easy to yell at the abyss and hear nothing but our own echoes. Walking through the valley of the shadow, who would lend a hand when I cried for help? To be told to pull myself together and cheer myself up is not that different from me advising someone who broke their leg to try getting up and walking, we have all been there.

I was concerned, I was worried and I was frightened. Interacting with people is usually not a pleasant experience for me, let alone doing that for six consecutive days. I was mindful of what my body was telling me, my heartbeat, my footsteps, and the bell had rung when I entered the room. It was quite unexpected, I did not panic, I did not make a fool of myself. It was surprisingly comforting to see each other in person, to cross paths with like-minded people who I would not have met otherwise, and to divulge things that I do not normally talk about. I am thankful that I get to voice out my feelings, without worrying about how others perceive me, I did not know that someone wants to hear our stories. Indeed, we have had our differences, and things turned out to be quite divergent from what many of us had anticipated. Nonetheless, the time spent meeting with our fellow warriors who have fought valiantly, and those who are eager to lend a hand, was fruitful.

Yes, we have taken our steps forward and we have won battles, but there is more to come, I have no doubt. If we wish to make a difference, there is so much more to be done. At present, I ponder the question of what needs to be done, so others do not have to face what I have gone through.

So much to learn

W. Crompton

I've worked the whole of my professional life in construction, specifically, as an electrician building airports. On the worksite, we're expected to suck it up, get in there and give 10 hours of hard work. In many ways I consider myself lucky. I enjoy my job and I have found some direction in my vocation. I studied aviation at university and now I get to build airports; it seems like a match made in heaven. Regrettably, in recent years, this has been overshadowed by the significant decline in my mental health. Long days of physical work and spending most of the year working in remote places away from friends, family and the things I enjoy doing has certainly taken its toll.

Suicide has been something that I've thought about since I was a young boy after years of being exposed to the idea that dying is an appropriate way to deal with emotional distress. Whether it be standing on a train station platform, looking nervously at the incoming train, or standing on top of a mountain looking over the edge, my mind is always thinking of the worst. Following a trip to the hospital in the back of a police car after threatening suicide, things have looked more positive since joining the Black Dog Institute team.

I became involved with Black Dog Institute in the capacity of a Lived Experience Advisor working on the co-design project 'Under the Radar', which aimed to gain a better understanding of why Australian men with thoughts of suicide are reluctant to consult traditional forms of mental health care. The goal was to create a new model of care that might be more appealing to this demographic. Participating in a research project that had a foundation in medical and social science but extended to include anecdotes and wisdom shared by other men with lived experience struggles was very enlightening and therapeutic. The process, however, was very convoluted, and I felt as though my insights were generalised, paraphrased or not considered altogether.

There is so much to learn from others who have walked the fine line between life and death; a perspective that cannot be captured through analysing statistics or asking Likert scale questions in a survey. Giving people with lived experience a voice can help to create real-world, life-changing outcomes; however, this can only be achieved if lived experience voices are genuinely listened to and considered by researchers. If not, the research outcome won't be a true reflection of the real needs of those experiencing mental distress.

Pay attention

N. Stevens

My involvement in the 'Under the Radar' programme has been a delightful experience for me as a suicide survivor. I welcome the interaction of staff and other men who like me have attempted suicide. The conversations are always very polite, and a little humour can from time to time find its way into the subject matter.

I feel privileged to be a member of the team and I sincerely hope that the knowledge being gained by the research being conducted by Black Dog Institute into the 'Under the Radar' group of men will be of value in years to come.

In more recent meetings, we have discussed the possibility of a contribution to a chapter of an upcoming book by the 'Under the Radar' group. I have noticed that of all the things mentioned, none have mentioned doctors, be they specialists or general practitioners.

I feel it is vitally important that the role of the medical profession and their involvement in the cause of suicide be addressed in this book. It is not a subject that can be approached lightly. Obviously, many medical professionals would be highly offended if one were to say "You played a significant role in my suicide attempt." In most cases rightly so.

However, let me tell my story. In short form if that is possible. My story actually begins in childhood. Being the second born of five, I was to become the whipping boy of my elder brother and my three sisters, a pair of twins among them.

Put simply, my elder brother learnt early in life that if he blamed me for something that occurred, he would be believed. Why? Because I was a very precocious child (I found out many years later I have a high level of intelligence). My mother and father were off a sugarcane farm in Northern Queensland, and both had left school by the age of 12. They had no idea how to deal with this child with a very inquiring mind. I quickly became known as the liar of the household, blame him and you will be believed.

So it was as the years went on that I became the child blamed with theft from mother's purse or taking some cake that was meant for afternoon tea, or whatever. At about age seven, my father introduced his police belt (he had become a policeman in Brisbane after injuring his back on the cane fields and no longer being able to cut cane) as part of the punishment for being a bad boy. These floggings would continue until at age 15, I took the police belt from him and threatened him with it. Whereupon I was told to get the fuck out of his house.

It was a year later when I left, after he said to "Cut your fucking hair or get out," but the clincher was, and I quote, "You are nothing but shit, you've always been shit, and you always will be shit." So I left. The thing is, I had endured years of floggings, constant harassment from my siblings, a mother who would say, and again I quote, "I never thought I could give birth to someone such as you. I didn't think it possible," meaning of course that she couldn't have given birth to someone as bad and awful as myself.

My childhood was horrific and in my early fifties I began to have nightmares about it. Slowly deteriorating over several years till at a point where my behaviour was becoming abnormal. Bouts of unnecessary anger, general grumpiness and depression. Insecurity growing by the day. I sought help.

This is where things went right and wrong. After seeking help and being started on medication, I finally settled on two meds that seemed to suit me. I must say, at one stage, I was taking five of one and two of the other. I was quite doped up. I lost interest in life and was quite a different person to the man I had been. Totally incapable of working and on a disability pension.

This went on for 12 years until in September 2020, I took 58 tablets I had saved up. I spent 24 hours in the Intensive Care Unit, 12 of those on life support. In the aftermath of the attempt, I quit medication altogether and as my wife says, "I have my husband back." But does she? After I had given up the meds and got a semblance of my old self back, I researched the medication I was taking for 12 years. BOTH were known to cause suicidal tendencies with prolonged use. There was also a physical disability caused by one of them, that is, a shrinkage of penile erection where the penis fully erect is about a third the size of the penis before taking the medication. No more sex for me.

Now it may be said that no one is at fault. Pardon me for not agreeing. The continued prescription of medication that causes suicidal tendencies is to me criminal in itself, if not just plain wrong. Indeed, not informing a patient over a 12-year period of the possible side effects of the medication they are taking is questionable at best. This should be addressed by the medical profession as a priority.

Up boy

Anonymous

> Up boy up lift your bloody chin
> You're no damn use unless you smile
> to your fellow and kin
> Give a wry smile give a cheeky wink
> and they will begin to think

he is a jolly fellow
One I would like to know
Never seems too troubled
Never seems too low

My only friend the end

Anonymous

Some are born to sweet delight
Some are born to endless night

This verse from 'Auguries of Innocence' by William Blake I think encapsulates my life. Others have sweet delight.

All my life I've been different, excessively shy, quiet and confused, I didn't identify with others.

I kept thinking I would have my day in the sun, but the nightmare continued. I didn't trust anyone, and on one occasion my mother told me, "Why did I have you?"

Was it meant? I don't know, but it contributed to my mental state.

I was sexually assaulted at age 13 by a religious teaching brother. I was an easy, vulnerable target, I didn't dare tell anyone.

I didn't really know what happened, except it was very wrong, confusion worsened, my parents really liked this guy.

Was I a gift from God to the world?

Not if you have any brains.

WHY?

Why was it my life decided on? Luck of the draw or roll of the dice?

I've never trusted anyone to my own detriment, costing me a real existence.

WHY?

I seemed

to become invisible to the world.

WHY?

I turned to the only true love of my life, ALCOHOL, and found relief therein, then GAMBLING my future away, but relief was there as well.

Bad days are when I lie in bed and think of things that might have been. The only answer was THE END.

Was I really alone? Just me?

WHY?

Why was I never noticed, even with doctors? No one cared.

BUT maybe other lost souls can help, aren't we all in this together? I'm starting to realise this could be true, I can get help that's been denied to me, not others' fault, just how my life was designed.

Time to come out of the shadows, there is time and help is available.
OR am I once again hoping for something that's not to be?

Be understanding towards me before trying to understand me

P. Sutton

To put it simply, be understanding towards me before trying to understand me.

$1 + 1 = ?$ Two is the answer you may say. I meant to say 1 apple + 1 orange $= ?$ You may say one apple and one orange. Or it could be two pieces of fruit.

If I cannot understand or explain my feelings, how can I explain them or answer the questions you ask?

Time, money and attitude are the missing links to help people rise out of the hole they are in.

Looking back at my lead up to attempting suicide highlights the previous sentence.

My belief is that to help people we need better training in listening and hearing. Society and some professionals still believe we need to toughen up. If we who are suffering could toughen up, do you not think we would?

Us struggling need to be heard in a non-judgemental, relaxed environment. When you are struggling with a reason to live, we need to feel the person we are talking to is willing to hear our story. Not to be looking for a diagnosis or a weakness in us.

It can take a long time and courage to open up honestly to somebody. To honestly hear us, gives us a reason to learn to trust you.

Helping me to sort through my destructive thoughts and start smothering the physical pain that can go with the frustration we feel.[1]

The people who are there to help us need to have the right attitude, education and experience. Only a few of the people I could speak to are suited to understand me. We are the ones who need help, not help to feel a failure or guilty that I cannot communicate my feelings and emotions rationally.

An open letter to the health-care workers of Australia

M. Whitten

Almost two years ago, I attempted to take my own life. The days leading up to my attempt and subsequent hospitalisation were undoubtedly the worst days of my life. If there was to be a silver lining in such a dark time, it was my willingness to reach out and participate in an enormous amount of support. This support has been pivotal to my road towards mental wellness. Support can come from many places, but for me it was medical professionals, clinical support, podcasts, group therapy, in-patient stays, participating in research studies, and the best support I found was finding other people just like me who have lived experience with suicide and mental health.

I wrote an open letter and sent it to every major news publication in Australia. I thought it was important to share my experience in the hope that health-care workers can take a moment to consider how my experience can be an example of how not to approach a patient who presents on what feels like the worst ever day of their life.

18 August 2020
An open letter to the health-care workers of Australia
The last seven days have been by far the worst days of my life. You see, I found myself at the very bottom rung of a long ladder and thought that the only option left was to take my own life. It was fortunate that an incredible team of health-care workers ensured that my physical wellbeing was superlatively cared for, I can't say the same for my mental wellbeing.

When I awoke the morning following my attempt, I was consumed with an enormous amount of shame and guilt. Still feeling the effects of the (way too many) painkillers I had ingested the night before, I knew that I needed medical and mental help. What I did was bad, this was going to be difficult to deal with.

I made my way to a private hospital. Upon arrival, I made it discretely known the reason why I had presented there. The first person in my journey thought it best to call out "We have a suicide attempt." Very quickly, nausea kicked in and I made my way outside to deal with this. Whilst outside, I was welcomed by the triage nurse who wondered why I wasn't answering her call in the waiting room, the vomit on my face, pants and ground was clearly not obvious.

The next comment was the trifecta[2] for how I was being treated: the triage nurse said, "You'd have been better off going to a 'public hospital' as they have a mental ward and can deal with you."

To be able to leave the hospital, there were two requirements: my liver was healthy, and I had met with a psychiatrist to assess my ability to return home and have the support I needed.

It took over 24 hours for the on-call psychiatrist to come and see me, a few questions were asked in-between answering the phone, text messages and saying hi to hospital employees walking past. During a very vulnerable moment, I did start to cry, the psychiatrist decided this would be the time to leave me to have a moment to myself. ... They never returned.

In case you are wondering, I did provide feedback to the hospital regarding my physical health and how the emergency team, triage team and on-call psychiatrist impacted on my already fragile mental health and wellbeing.

No response yet has been provided, disappointed.

Art is my voice

C. Clerke (artist)

Figure 4.1: 'Punching in a Dream'

I am a recovering addict, six years clean and sober, yet a long way to walk out of the woods I found myself lost in. I spent 25 years of my life addicted to escaping reality and the feelings that came with it.

I come here with a lived experience of trauma. Of childhood abuse, suicidal ideation, intentional overdoses, failed attempts at suicide and the shame I once felt around it.

And I have art. 'A voice that speaks a language my words cannot.'

I am a self-taught, self-proclaimed Punk-Pop artist living in a contemporary art world.

I share these artworks for the beautiful men in our group. Our struggles, our pain and our trauma.

I share this with the knowledge that when we recover loudly, we keep others from dying quietly. You are not alone, you are loved.

My first piece, 'Punching in a Dream' (Figure 4.1) highlights the internal struggle from within that is mental health. Silent on the exterior but screaming for relief on the inside. I used to walk around a local park on some really dark days blaring a song that summed up the way I felt at the time.

> Bright lights turn me green, this is worse than it seems,
> Wait, I don't ever want to be here,
> Like punching in a dream, breathing life into my nightmare.
> (Lyrics by the Naked and Famous)

I often paint things that I can't convey into words. My second piece, 'PURGE ... restore my soul' (Figure 4.2), is the epitome of that. The shards of glass violently spewing from the eye sockets represent the sharp, brittle pieces of life that, once rid of, will no longer pain you and the prescribed formulas being dopamine, oxytocin and serotonin – the mental cocktail.

It's a work in progress letting it all go, ridding myself of demons, the chaos, purging the shit that doesn't serve me. And it's an ongoing process, one that for me at times seems agonisingly slow. I guess it's the aftermath of an earlier piece titled 'Billy Gnosis' (Figure 4.3).

I composed this work just after leaving rehab in Bali, well, after I got kicked out of rehab. I played a song called 'Billy Gnosis' by Bad Religion on repeat the whole flight back to Oz. It highlights the chaos wreaking havoc in my unbalanced mind and the visions I had which portrays that.

Figure 4.2: 'PURGE ... restore my soul'

Figure 4.3: 'Billy Gnosis'

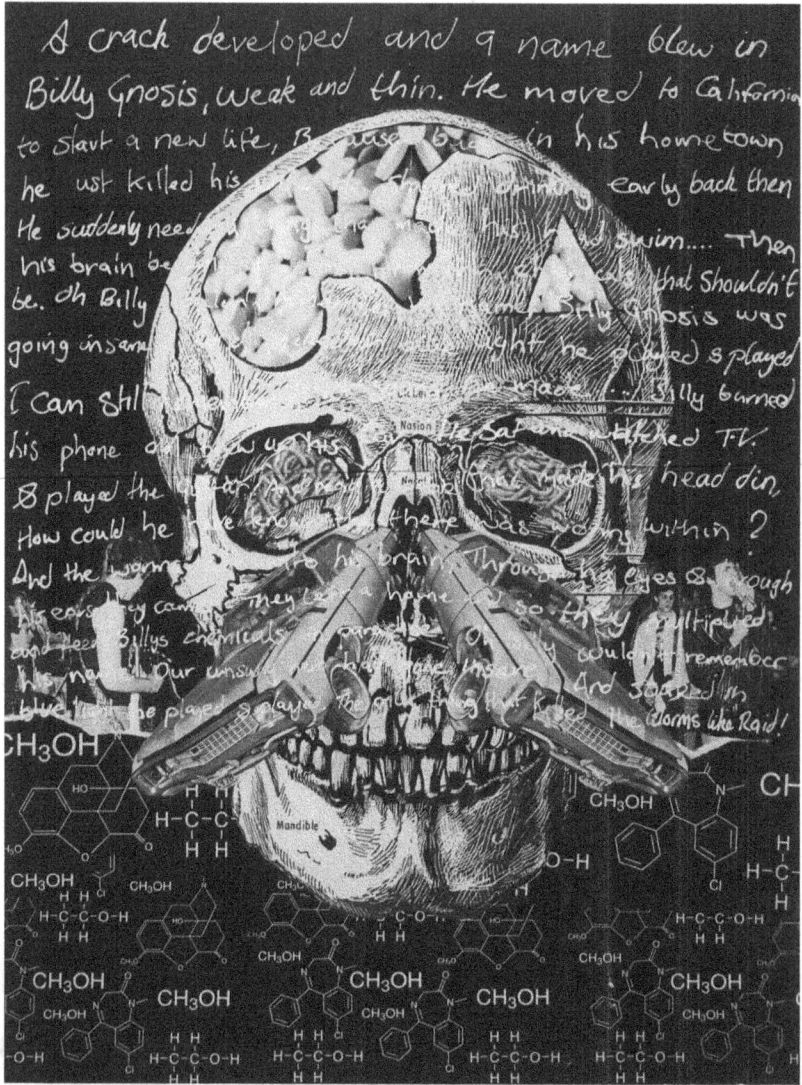

Oubliette

S. Lake

Stephen's poem attempts to convey the experience of an entire life lived with the experience and effects of trauma, with recurring suicide attempts and ideation, incarcerated in a society within which he feels misunderstood and unable to breathe. The iconography of Saint Sebastian (see Figure 4.4) reflects for him a sense in which society destroys its own members; the hand that willingly takes one's own life, humanity, individuality, potential, is held by others.

Figure 4.4: *Saint Sebastian*, painted by Gerrit van Honthurst (1592–1656)

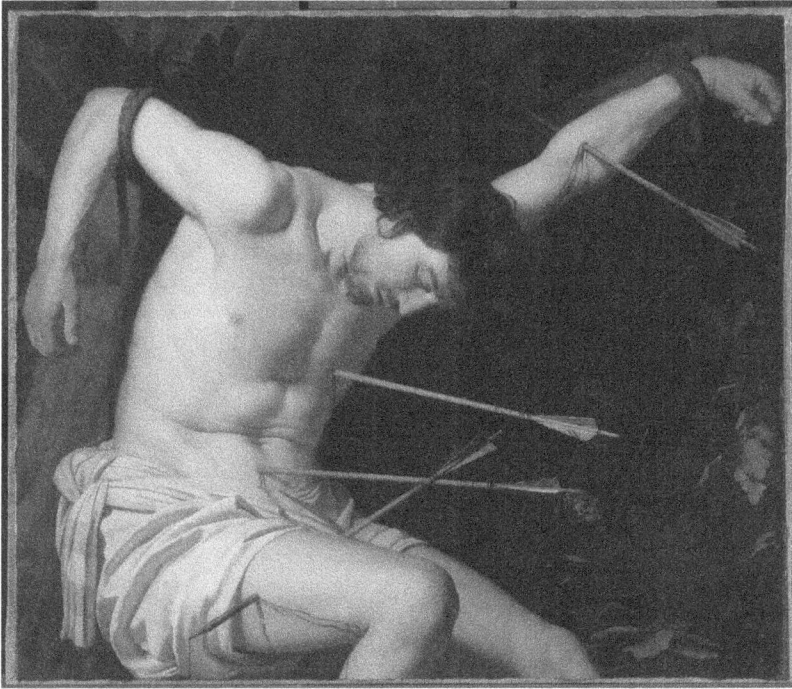

Source: The National Gallery, London

Washed upon a sterile shore by birth
On which footprints are erased, hands grasp only emptiness
A scream annulled in the mere nothingness of silence
An ageless pulsing cicatrice, leprosy of a tattooed number

Endless sky of magnificent textures ceaselessly transforming
Translucent kaleidoscopic, overwhelmed in infernal darkness
Voices arise of other selves within, at once possessing and possessed
Alternating hope and throbbing despair irreconcilable

My tongues are unintelligible amidst this wasteland
Void here of visions and meaning
Alone by seeking refuge beneath other skies, in other lands, other times
Will this silence be shattered, yet inescapably we bear our prisons with us

Nostalgia for labyrinthine illusions, dreams of other lives no more
Than wistful glances through windows of distorting glass

Whispers of redeeming love evaded, memories unfulfilled
Inchoate desire for the barren fertility denied

Divine sparks of soul metamorphose into demonic grimaces
Incessant bartering between promise and the curse imposed
Until exhaustion becomes in flesh what spirit always was
Another All Souls beyond the eternal shelter of a Madonna's mantle

Dusk over snowed heights, no more a dawn ambivalent
Pale light through bare branches fragmented
This solitary path leads not home to some warming hearth
But only to a sarcophagus upon an unmarked plinth.

Conclusion

This writing project involved important conversations about lived experience engagement that prompted co-design of a Lived Experience Engagement Framework. The Framework acts as a central resource providing guidance for anyone at Black Dog seeking to engage effectively and safely with people with a lived or living experience of mental health challenges and/or suicidality, their carers and support people. While there are several publicly available frameworks for engagement with people with lived and living experience in the mental health sector, as a medical research institute, this framework was developed to ensure that we are adhering to Black Dog Institute values in a consistent, best practice approach which supports our staff and people with lived and/or living experience working together.

Lived Experience Advisors need to be fully involved from the inception of a co-design project, to feel that they have equal agency within the process and to be communicated with in terms that are meaningful to them. It would have been useful for all involved had each of the men with lived experience had an opportunity at the outset to tell their own stories to the team members. Where an outcome is de facto pre-determined, or the process is controlled by the team and Lived Experience Advisors are not sufficiently heard, no project is co-designed. Inherent in lived experience engagement is a power imbalance, which unequivocally exists between people for whom services or interventions are intended, and those who develop these outputs. Therefore, establishing collaboration with people with lived experience requires an active re-balancing of such power, by elevating their lived experience knowledge as equal with the complementary knowledge and skills of mental health teams.

The research basis used to inform any project should be sufficiently broad as to identify and utilise all relevant publications. It should be used to educate team members, particularly where they do not have qualifications and experience in the field, and such research should be critically evaluated to identify methodological flaws and lacunae in what may still need to be further investigated. 'Research' is not infallible.

With respect to mental health and suicide, the education, training, practice and attitudes of psychologists, general practitioners and psychiatrists need to be re-assessed, as there are multiple limitations. Lived Experience Advisors and professionals each have areas of unique insight or knowledge, but any such expertise is finite, not omniscient. The challenge of a co-design project is to enable those insights and that knowledge to *both* shape the processes and outcomes equally and where necessary to challenge dominant paradigms. Without understanding what it is like to be in the skin of people with lived experience, and how best to address that experience, no response is likely to be widely effective. Many factors predisposing people to suicide are outside the immediate purview of the mental health sector, such that a whole-of-society, social justice approach is required, supported by advocacy by mental health professionals and those with lived experience communicating to government.

Acknowledgements

The authors would like to express their grateful appreciation to Professor Katherine Boydell, Black Dog Institute, who invited them to write these contributions, and Emma Elder and Nyree Gale, who supported them throughout this process.

Notes

[1] The author intentionally widens the subject from the individual to the group halfway through this sentence. This has two functions. First, it is inclusive/creates community as the feeling is not an isolated one but a shared experience of frustration; second, it creates distance between the person and the feeling of frustration.

[2] 'Trifecta' is a colloquialism the author uses to emphasise three separate instances of discrimination/abuse he experiences in one hospital admission.

Further reading

Dreier, M., Baumgardt, J., Bock, T., Härter, M., The 8 Lives Team and Liebherz, S. (2021) 'Development of an online suicide prevention program involving people with lived experience: Ideas and challenges', *Research Involvement and Engagement*, 7(60): 1–14.

Gan, D.Z.Q., McGillivray, L., Larsen, M.E., Bloomfield, T. and Torok, M. (2023) 'Promoting engagement with Smartphone apps for suicidal ideation in young people: Development of an adjunctive strategy using a lived experience participatory design approach', *JMIR Formative Research*, 7(e45234).

Schlichthorst, M., Ozols, I., Reifels, L. and Morgan, A. (2020) 'Lived experience peer support programs for suicide prevention: A systematic scoping review', *International Journal of Mental Health Systems*, 14(65): 1–12.

Shamsaei F., Yaghmaei S. and Haghighi M. (2020) 'Exploring the lived experiences of the suicide attempt survivors: A phenomenological approach', *International Journal of Qualitative Studies on Health and Well-being*, 15(1745478): 1–9.

References

Al-Halabí, S. and Fonseca-Pedrero, E. (ed) (2023) *Manual de psicología de la conducta suicida*, Madrid: Ediciones Pirámide.

Australian Bureau of Statistics (2020) 'Intentional self-harm deaths (Suicide) in Australia', *Causes of Death, Australia*. Available from: https://www.abs.gov.au/statistics/health/causes-death/causes-death-australia/latest-release#intentional-self-harm-deaths-suicide-in-australia [Accessed 24 June 2022].

Battin, M.P. (ed) (2015) *The Ethics of Suicide: Historical Sources*, Oxford: Oxford University Press.

Bell, G. (2005) 'The worried well: The depression epidemic and the medicalisation of our sorrows', *Quarterly Essay*, 18, Melbourne: Black Inc.

Case, A. and Deaton, A. (2020) *Deaths of Despair and the Future of Capitalism*, Princeton: Princeton University Press.

Durkheim, É. (1897) *Le suicide. Étude de sociologie*, Paris: Presses Universitaires de France, 2013 edition.

Halbwachs, M. (1930) *Les causes du suicide*, Paris: Presses Universitaires de France, 2002 edition.

Herman, J. (2015) *Trauma and Recovery: The Aftermath of Violence – From Domestic Violence to Political Terror* (2nd edn), New York: Basic Books.

Horowitz, M. and Moncrieff, J. (2022) 'Chemical imbalance theory of depression: clearing up some misconceptions', *The Conversation*. Available from: https://theconversation.com/chemical-imbalance-theory-of-depression-clearing-up-some-misconceptions-188921 [Accessed 24 August 2022]

Jamison, K.R. (1999) *Night Falls Fast: Understanding Suicide*, New York: Vintage Books.

Johnston, A.K., Pirkis, J.E. and Burgess, P.M. (2009) 'Suicidal thoughts and behaviours among Australian adults: Findings from the 2007 National Survey of Mental Health and Wellbeing', *Australian and New Zealand Journal of Psychiatry*, 43(7): 635–643.

Krasnostein, S. (2022) 'Drowning, not waving: Mental illness and vulnerability in Australia', *Quarterly Essay*, 85(1): 1–23.

Masaryk, T.G. (1881) *Der Selbstmord als sociale Massenerscheinung der modernen Civilisation*, Vienna: Carl Konegen Verlag.

Murray, A. (1998) *Suicide in the Middle Ages*, Volume 1: *The violent against themselves*, Oxford: Oxford University Press.

Murray, A. (2000) *Suicide in the Middle Ages, Volume 2: The curse on self-murder*, Oxford: Oxford University Press.

Paperny, A.M. (2020) *Hello I Want to Die Please Fix Me: Depression in the First Person*, New York: The Experiment.

Schopenhauer, A. (1859) *Die Welt als Wille und Vorstellung* (3rd edn), Munich: Deutscher Taschenbuch Verlag.

Stene-Larsen, K. and Reneflot, A. (2019) 'Contact with primary and mental health care prior to suicide: A systematic review of the literature from 2000 to 2017', *Scandinavian Journal of Public Health*, 47(1): 9–17.

Tang, S., Reily, N., Arena, A., Batterham, P., Calear, A., Carter, G., Mackinnon, A. and Christensen, H. (2022) 'People who die by suicide without receiving mental health services: A systematic review', *Frontiers in Public Health*, 9(12): 1–12.

Van Der Kolk, B. (2014) *The Body Keeps the Score: Mind, Brain and Body in the Transformation of Trauma*, London: Penguin Books.

5

Co-researching with persons with disabilities: reflections and lessons learned

Chrysant Lily Kusumowardoyo, Husna Yuni Wulansari, Irmansyah Songgoua, Elias Katapi, Zainab and Yassin Ali Hadu

Key points

- This chapter disrupts the academy by providing intersectional perspectives on the tensions and strengths of research collaborations with persons with disabilities, based on research in Indonesia.
- Establishing an equal collaborative relationship can be challenging especially due to the inherent power imbalance with co-researchers. It is important to be aware of and acknowledge this openly, and jointly work together to resolve such issues.
- The full participation of persons with disabilities should be a key concern throughout all stages of research production. However, limited time and resources, especially for a short-term research project, could be a major constraint in achieving this goal.
- Reasonable accommodation, accessibility and sharing of research knowledge and practical skills are indispensable to support the participation of persons with disabilities, especially in complex settings such as disaster research.
- By establishing trust and well-coordinated processes with co-researchers, we can constantly reflect on and improve our methods in conducting research.

Introduction

Persons with disabilities face higher disaster risks, for instance, due to the inaccessibility of disaster preparedness information, evacuation shelter and relief assistance. Structural inequalities also mean that many do not have the resources to cope with a disaster (Twigg et al, 2018). Understanding the experiences of persons with disabilities before, during and after a disaster is important to inform efforts in reducing and managing such risks. Thus, the participation of persons with disabilities in disaster research as experts with lived experience is crucial (Gartrell et al, 2020). However, research focused on the experiences of persons with disabilities in disasters has only emerged in recent decades, significantly later than research on the experiences of other at-risk groups such as children, women, disadvantaged and Indigenous minorities (Stough and Kelman, 2018).

Further, the role of persons with disabilities in disaster research has been limited to being research subjects, that is, where research is done *on* them rather than *by* or *with* them (Ollerton, 2012). Consequently, persons with disabilities are alienated from the research process and have no say in shaping the direction of the research nor benefit from knowledge production (Kitchin, 2000).

For at least three decades, disability scholars have criticised this unequal relationship in research production (Oliver, 1992; Zarb, 1992; Stone and Priestley, 1996) based on the 'social model of disability' (see Shakespeare, 2006). The model is reflected in the description of 'persons with disabilities' in the Convention on the Rights of Persons with Disabilities, as 'those who have long-term physical, mental, intellectual, or sensory impairments in which interaction with various barriers may hinder their full and effective participation in society on an equal basis with others' (United Nations, 2008: 4). Based on this model, the focus of research should be on various social barriers that create the experience of disablement, instead of on the impairment as the individual 'problem'. These barriers include:

- 'physical barriers' such as inaccessible infrastructures and facilities;
- 'attitudinal barriers' such as stigma, stereotypes and discrimination towards persons with disabilities;
- 'communicational barriers' such as inaccessible information and technology; and
- 'institutional barriers' which includes laws, policies and procedures that systematically marginalise persons with disabilities.

Furthermore, central to the critique is the effort to challenge the traditional power relations between researchers and 'the researched'. Instead of further alienating persons with disabilities, research should be an empowering experience for them where researchers with no lived experience collaborate with persons with disabilities in a participatory manner (Balcazar et al, 2006). Based on this understanding, we define collaborative research as a joint project based on a sense of trust, shared responsibility, mutual benefits and ownership among the disability and non-disability researchers involved, to participate and bring a unique contribution that complements one another. In such a relationship, no one is above the other, and everyone has an equal opportunity to collectively shape the research direction.

However, achieving full participation and equal collaborative partnerships between disability and non-disability researchers is not a straightforward process (Kusumowardoyo and Wulansari, 2022). Each have intersectional identities that uniquely shape their experience of disempowerment and privilege. These realities bring certain complexities in shifting power relations among non-disability researchers and co-researchers who are persons with disabilities. In this chapter, we use collaborative autoethnography (see Chapter 1) to share reflections on our experiences of co-production of research in a post-disaster context in Central Sulawesi, Indonesia.

We reflected on the question of 'who participates' because 'disability' is not a homogeneous category. Certain types of impairments continue to be under-represented among 'persons with disabilities', including invisible or hidden impairments as well as impairments people are unwilling to discuss openly. In Indonesia, certain kinds of disabilities are still hidden and heavily stigmatised in the community. When undertaking this project, we had no established experience or capacity to work with persons with 'invisible' disabilities. As this was a short-term research project, it was unrealistic for us to set up a partnership from scratch with organisations that work with persons with invisible disabilities. Therefore, the reflections in this chapter might not address the specific lived experiences of persons with invisible disabilities.

Our collaborative research took place in 2020–2021, focusing on the inclusion of older persons and persons with disabilities in the water, sanitation and hygiene response following the earthquake, tsunami and liquefaction that struck Central Sulawesi in late 2018. Three organisations were involved in this research:

1. Arbeiter-Samariter-Bund Indonesia and the Philippines (ASB), an international humanitarian organisation that focuses on inclusive disaster preparedness and response;
2. Center for Health Policy and Management (CHPM), a research agency of the University of Gadjah Mada Indonesia; and
3. the Working Group of Organisations of Persons with Disabilities in Central Sulawesi.

The Working Group is a federation of four local organisations for persons with disabilities in the area, namely Perkumpulan Penyandang Disabilitas Indonesia (PPDI, Indonesian Association of People with Disabilities), Persatuan Tuna Netra Indonesia (Pertuni, Indonesian Blind Association), Himpunan Wanita Disabilitas Indonesia (HWDI, Indonesian Women with Disabilities Association) and Gerakan untuk Kesejahteraan Tuna Rungu Indonesia (Gerkatin, Movement for Indonesian Deaf Peoples Welfare). The Working Group of Persons with Disabilities was established during the early response phase to ensure representation of different disability groups in humanitarian coordination mechanisms.

The following processes guided our co-creation of knowledge through collaborative research:

- ASB and CHPM developed the research design, methods and protocols, and secured ethical clearance. The interview guide was translated into a local language (Kaili), printed in Braille, and adapted into an easy-to-read format with pictures.
- ASB selected persons with disabilities to take part in the research based on their interest and commitment to be co-researchers and a balanced representation of gender and types of impairments. A total of 18 members (eight women, ten men) were selected.
- ASB and CHPM facilitated training on water, sanitation and hygiene topics, and the research methodology and methods. Co-researchers familiarised themselves with the interview guide through in-class and field testing.
- ASB created teams consisting of two co-researchers. They were responsible for coordinating with local village officials and identifying potential informants in each location (nine villages in three subdistricts). They made a further selection based on eligibility criteria.
- In pairs, nine groups of co-researchers conducted semi-structured interviews with eligible informants in each location. They interviewed 29 persons with disabilities (14 women, 15 men) and 30 older people (18 women, 12 men).
- ASB transcribed and analysed the data and organised a validation workshop with co-researchers and informants.
- ASB and co-researchers wrote the research report and the guidelines on co-researching with persons with disabilities (see Further reading section), and with CHPM, organised several dissemination activities to share these outcomes.

We shared tasks as we wanted the collaboration to be based on the strengths and expertise that each partner could bring to the co-research process. For instance, since co-researchers were based in their research location and were also affected by the disaster, they were responsible to collect data from persons with disabilities. Since ASB had access to a network of humanitarian actors, it was responsible for data collection from the latter. Similarly, CHPM was mainly responsible for the design, protocols and methods, and for obtaining ethical clearance, as these were its areas of expertise. While this arrangement was practical and helped the collaboration to be efficient, ASB, as the project lead, decided on the arrangement based on assumptions regarding the interest and capacities of co-researchers. We reflect on how this affected our collaboration later.

There are six writers in this chapter: Chrysant and Husna (non-disability researchers from ASB), and Irmansyah, Elias, Zainab and Yassin who were Chrysant and Husna's co-researchers. Elias is a male Blind person from Pertuni, Yassin is a male Deaf person from Gerkatin, while Irmansyah (male) and Zainab (female) are persons with mobility difficulties from PPDI and HWDI respectively. They mostly work as unpaid volunteers. During the research, Chrysant and Husna worked full-time as Partnership Manager and Research Officer respectively. They had the privilege of representing a lead organisation with direct access to the donor (Elrha's Humanitarian Innovation Fund). As ASB's office is in Yogyakarta, Western Indonesia, Chrysant and Husna enjoyed better access to public facilities compared to co-researchers and research participants who live in Eastern Indonesia, a less developed part of the country.

Chrysant and Husna speak Indonesian as well as different local languages. They communicated with co-researchers using Indonesian but relied on co-researchers to communicate with research participants in local languages. Chrysant and Husna both had the privilege of accessing higher education and working with academics, which gave them the experience of learning research methodologies and conducting research. Considering our different backgrounds, we thought it would be useful to share our different positionalities before presenting the conversation we had via videoconferencing meetings over three months (March–May 2022) to develop this chapter.

The videoconferencing meetings were chosen as a method for our joint writing as we were located on different islands in Indonesia, and co-researchers had no devices such as laptops to support their writing. Chrysant and Husna asked questions regarding previous co-research experiences to each co-author in separate meetings to ensure that everyone would feel comfortable talking about any topic. Chrysant and Husna developed questions based on the suggested outline of the chapter provided by the book editors and distributed these before online meetings. Each interview was recorded, and Chrysant and Husna coded the transcripts and grouped prominent themes.

Chrysant and Husna wrote their sections in English and translated sections by Irmansyah, Elias, Zainab and Yassin from Indonesian into English. These sections were combined into one narrative. We share our reflections on collaboration and research co-production, and on the impact of our collaboration. We conclude by sharing key takeaways for applying our approach in other contexts.

Our collaboration processes

What did we wish to achieve through co-research?

Persons with disabilities are actively involved in research

Chrysant: For too long, persons with disabilities have been the object of various kinds of research only as passive informants. By learning how to conduct research, I hope that research will no longer be something distant for our partners who are persons with disabilities. This means that, in the future, they already know about researchers' responsibilities and can demand that all researchers conduct research ethically. I was hoping that from our collaboration, co-researchers would gain practical research knowledge and experience to enable them to conduct their research in the future. That way, we can change the paternalistic relationship where researchers 'give voice', but rather, persons with disabilities themselves actively produce research and 'take voice' through authorship (Kelman and Stough, 2015).

Husna: I wanted to learn from our partners with disabilities as they are experts in disability inclusion. I wanted to better understand how we can ensure everyone participates meaningfully in research activities, how to design and implement research methods that can accommodate the needs and preferences of co-researchers with disabilities, and how non-disability researchers can be more adaptable in facilitating learning and sharing among all of us.

I was hoping that the research processes could support co-researchers to voice their concerns on our collaboration. In my opinion, this collaboration should make them feel encouraged to be more active in shaping the direction of research activities, even though back then they felt like they were not 'skilful' or 'experienced' enough to become researchers. I was also hoping that this co-research could be evidence for other humanitarian practitioners and scholars that Persons with Disabilities can participate in or lead research when they get the support they need to overcome barriers.

Persons with disabilities can meaningfully participate in all stages of research

Elias: My wish is that in the future, if you want to do research, it should involve people with disabilities or older people. They should be invited to participate fully and be active in all research design activities.

Irmansyah: From the beginning of the process to the end, if it is possible, we should be involved. As people with disabilities, there are things we want to research, even though we may have limitations.

Zainab: I wish that we, co-researchers with disabilities, could be directly involved in research planning so that we can also share our experiences with others with disabilities who are not involved in the research activity. Some of my colleagues ... when invited to join project-related activities, they feel ... and say "I can't" because they've never been involved in any activity. So, we want to motivate our colleagues who have not been involved.

What worked well and why?

Previous collaboration with, and existing capacity, of co-researchers with disabilities

Chrysant: The research was not the first collaboration between ASB and Persons with Disabilities. Through a joint humanitarian response in 2018, there was already an existing relationship. ASB had some ideas about the needs and capacities of Persons with Disabilities, and the latter had seen our commitment to upholding disability inclusion in our work. There was also some level of trust, which is a very important foundation for further collaboration in research. Another aspect that I think went well in terms of our collaboration is that both ASB and co-researchers mutually benefited from the relationship. The mutual relationship where each partner contributes something based on their expertise and gains a certain benefit from such collaborations is key to creating more equal relationships among disability and non-disability researchers, a relationship that is not exploitative and extractive.

Yassin: When I interviewed older persons and informants with disabilities, I did not feel so worried, because I have previous interviewing experience. Before this research, there was a programme for data collection on disabilities (during disasters). At that time, we did the interviews as well.

Research training and preparation activities support the collaborative processes

Irmansyah: The training was very useful ... through the process of both online training and in-class training, it allowed us to do research ... to practice data collection in the field, this made it easier for us to do research activities later.

Reasonable accommodation and coordination could support participation of Persons with Disabilities

Irmansyah: ASB, in terms of the collaboration, has of course provided transportation, then built rapport with the village government so these governments would welcome the activities carried out by ASB and Persons with Disabilities. Then in the research locations, we stayed coordinated, for example, in collecting data. Afterwards, we sat together again to discuss. Then we did some kind of evaluation. We discussed obstacles from the field and what worked well. So that's the collaboration with ASB, it's a solid team.

Elias: ASB is willing to involve persons with disabilities to join the research despite the limited circumstances. It's great that ASB is willing to take the risk, such as providing for our necessities. For example, I needed a recording device and a Braille research instrument. ASB generally understood the needs of co-researchers in the collaboration ... we have been facilitated with accommodation, including vehicles and technical assistance for doing research.

Zainab: I think ASB has prepared well, [they understood] our needs for data collection, mobility, the tools that we brought for the research. ... Like stationery, the question forms, and a recording device for conducting interviews. ... We were equipped with a mask, sanitiser and face shield.

Persons with Disabilities managed to successfully collect data and build rapport with the informants

Irmansyah: We were able to read the situations. When informants did not understand the questions, then we tried to make them more understandable in the simplest possible way. ... We were able to adapt to the environment and new things, and we could interact and communicate well.

Husna: Despite the different challenges each group faced in their research locations, co-researchers managed to use the knowledge and skills from the training – which was done in quite a short period. I went to Central Sulawesi to assist them with data collection, and based on my observations, they were successful in interviewing informants. They did a great job in probing, paraphrasing and explaining complicated questions, and creating a safe and comfortable situation for the informants to share their experiences during disasters. This is a valuable achievement which I think resulted from co-researchers' initiatives to always ask questions, give input, and clarify whenever our training materials, learning sessions and research instruments were difficult to understand. Their desire to keep learning has led us to collaborate well and to constantly reflect on our methods in facilitating their participation.

What was challenging and why?

Navigating the imbalance of power relations between ASB and Persons with Disabilities

Chrysant: For me achieving an equal partnership where both partners have equal opportunity for joint decision-making is challenging. Since ASB is the project lead, there is an inherent imbalance of power between ASB and co-researchers. ASB is the one with access to the donor's fund and is in charge of allocating resources to support the participation of persons with disabilities in research. This includes providing a daily allowance, transportation costs, mobile data reimbursement for participation in online activities, and other types of reasonable accommodation.

ASB is also responsible for ensuring smooth project management to ensure accountability to our donors, and as a result, we often have to make decisions based on practicalities to ensure that the project progresses within the agreed timeline. For instance, considering that Persons with Disabilities must have a wide network nationally, we decided that other Persons with Disabilities organisations should be the target of our research dissemination activities. We did not consider or even consult with co-researchers about whether there were other stakeholders that they thought were important to them. Such 'shortcuts' in decision-making were made because we were under time constraints.

Zainab: Husna once accompanied me during the interview process. Honestly, this made me nervous. As someone with a disability, I am so used to being undermined by others, even my family members. It's like they're expecting that I will fail and won't even be able to finish primary school. When Husna decided to observe my group instead of others during the interview, I took it as the same sign of distrust ... that she didn't believe I knew how to put words together and thought I would fail. I realise this might not be the case, but that was my first reaction because of my past experience. But then, as I did in the past, I chose to show that I can do it. I finished not only primary school but junior high. In the data collection, I showed Husna that I know how to simplify and specify the interview questions, to probe for answers. I learnt from her comments during our data collection process.

Husna: During data collection, I took turns accompanying different co-researcher teams in interviewing informants. Sometimes it was hard for me to navigate my role as a research officer who was responsible for monitoring and ensuring data quality while making sure that they have the power to lead data collection. I tried to convey constructive feedback or comments regarding their interview methods when necessary. However, I also felt that co-researchers were being more 'cautious' in interviewing informants when I was around them. I guess my position as ASB staff has inevitably made them feel like they were being supervised. Meanwhile, I also wanted to create a situation where they could enjoy the process as an opportunity to learn, instead of being pressured to gain perfect results.

Accessibility issues due to environmental and communicational barriers experienced during data collection

Irmansyah: As a wheelchair user, the challenge is that there are some informants whose houses were inaccessible for wheelchair users. … But because of our fighting spirit, we want to learn; in this data collection and research what was important for us is that we try to collaborate well with our teammates as well.

Zainab: In one situation, the informant did not understand sign language, meanwhile Sadri [Zainab's teammate] used his sign language [to communicate]. That is because at that time, there was only one sign language interpreter involved and she was accompanying another Deaf co-researcher.

Yassin: During interviews … in Sigi, it was challenging because there were many difficult words, so it was difficult to understand. Some terms were in English, and those terms were hard to interpret or visualise … and the Deaf informants did not use a similar sign language as I do …

they use a different kind of sign language, like a 'natural' language. So, when I communicated using Bisindo [Indonesian sign language], they found it difficult to understand, [there were] many miscommunications. Some Deaf informants did not go to school. ... So, their words were very difficult to understand.

Language barriers

Irmansyah: A challenge emerged because ASB only translated the interview questions into one kind of Kaili language [Kaili is the local language in Central Sulawesi and there are multiple versions of Kaili depending on the area].

Elias: Here in Central Sulawesi, there are several languages ... the local languages have different dialects, concepts and usages, and this was not captured and understood by [the organisations].

Zainab: The difficulty I experienced during data collection was that some informants could not understand the languages we used to communicate, so we had to keep explaining the terms [in the interview questions]. I am very sensitive about making our communication as accessible as possible because as someone with a disability, I have experienced situations where I attended meetings and events and had difficulty following the discussion since they used complicated terms. It made me feel excluded. From those experiences, I learned to choose simple words that are easy to understand so I don't exclude informants with disabilities in the villages.

Impact and outcomes of the collaboration

What were the things that we consider as the impacts of our collaboration?

Impacts on the organisational or project level

Chrysant: We were able to push the boundaries regarding the common perception about the relationship between persons with disabilities and research. We have successfully demonstrated that in research, persons with disabilities can actively produce knowledge as co-researchers.

Husna: The collaboration has shown that co-researchers with disabilities have experienced some improvements in conducting research, especially in data collection and dissemination processes. This project has produced evidence that it is possible to actively involve persons with disabilities as co-researchers, as long as the research planning and budgeting enables participatory methods.

Impacts on the personal level

Chrysant: On a personal level, I think the impact of our collaborations is that I became aware of my biases as someone without disability. Although I believe in the capacity of persons with disabilities, I still have certain assumptions about what they can or cannot do. For instance, I know that co-researchers never had formal training in research skills. I figured that it would be easier for them to simply become enumerators instead of interviewers. As enumerators, they can simply read out the answer options to research participants, while as interviewers, they would need to have probing skills, which I assumed would be harder for them. I did not realise that I had this undermining attitude until much later, after we had decided to have the co-researchers with disabilities do interviews and after they demonstrated that they can develop the necessary skills – proving that my assumptions about their capacity were wrong. It is only from the experience of collaborating like this that I had such an eye-opening realisation about my biases.

Husna: This collaboration made me aware of the complexities of collaborating with persons with disabilities. We might have this ideal goal in mind to be fully inclusive and participatory from the research design phase, but limited time and resources were the biggest challenges in realising our goal. I also became more adaptable in facilitating any research process with partners with disabilities. I have learned to practice active listening and constantly reflect on my work and positionality as a non-disability researcher. One of my main takeaways is that to some extent, this collaboration still relied on some top-down mechanism in which the non-disability researchers, who *relatively* have more research experience, had more power in deciding what to do, when and how. This is not ideal, of course. But we have learned a lot from this collaboration. It will certainly require a longer-term strategy to cultivate equal partnership in the future.

Irmansyah: From the research experiences, we could do many positive things ... for example, we can adapt to the new environment, we can communicate well, so there's some kind of confidence boost. ... We could also interact with other persons with disabilities, and motivate our friends to get involved, to learn together with us, those who have been involved and have experiences.

Elias: I have managed to speak in public. Honestly, back then, when I had not been involved, I was not able to talk about the water, sanitation and hygiene services in *huntara* [temporary shelter] when the disaster occurred. We could not speak in public because we did not have the knowledge and capacity ... so I also feel more confident.

Zainab: There is an added value for me personally. For example, after this research, people in my village can see that I have the capacity in this field. They involve me in LPM [Lembaga Pemberdayaan Masyarakat/Community Empowerment Agency] at the village level. That means the communities do not only consider me as a person with disabilities. They also see that I have strength in this field, in seeing and understanding the local situation in the village, therefore I am involved.

How did we evaluate our practices?

We applied some evaluation processes during the research collaboration

Chrysant: We used several methods to evaluate the impacts of the research project on the knowledge improvement of co-researchers – for instance, the Knowledge, Attitude and Practice survey that we used at the beginning and the end of the project, the pre/post-test to measure knowledge before and after the training, quizzes during training, and so on. We used observations regarding how well co-researchers put their knowledge into practice. We also measured the learning outcomes by reviewing the learning diary that co-researchers filled out after the training sessions and data collection. The learning diary asked them to reflect and document what they learned, skills or knowledge they felt they developed and how they plan to use them in the future, and what they did well or would like to improve.

We relied on feedback from the post-activity evaluation where we invited co-researchers to share what went well and what needed to be improved in terms of the way we organised a certain activity, such as training. Through the learning diary, we asked them to share their opinions regarding this event. The feedback we received was mainly positive, and to validate the results by the end of the project, we invited an external facilitator to collect feedback about the collaboration.

Husna: I think it required a deeper and more constant interaction with co-researchers to get their feedback. Some preferred to be approached individually rather than to speak up in a group setting when it came to collecting feedback. There were also some informal situations such as during lunch breaks or informal conversations outside of work settings where some co-researchers felt more comfortable sharing their concerns and criticism.

How did we know when things were working?

There was positive feedback from co-researchers

Chrysant: We knew that things were working because there was no conflict, no indication of dissatisfaction that co-researchers had towards our collaboration, and the feedback was overwhelmingly positive. Yet, we did not know whether the positive feedback was because of the unequal power relationship, because we may not come across as serious enough in wanting feedback, or because co-researchers are simply not used to reflecting on their collaboration with others. I think there is a risk that in a world where you are repeatedly denied the opportunity to be involved and to collaborate in anything, it is so easy to have low expectations when a collaborative relationship exists. Hence, the feedback we often receive are things along the lines of, "We're happy with our collaboration and we appreciate ASB for working with us."

Husna: Yes, the absence of negative feedback does not necessarily prove that the collaboration is working. Some co-researchers already have the influence and capacity to be more openly critical of our practices, while the others (perhaps) are still in the process of getting used to conveying their feedback. There were moments when some co-researchers personally shared their concerns about research activities, and these moments happened outside of formal settings.

There is a sense of mutual trust

Zainab: As I recall, Husna didn't correct the results of the data collection I had done in that village too much ... Husna only accompanied me once. It means that Husna has given me a lot of trust to do it myself.

There is a concrete deliverable of the collaboration

Zainab: I think it went well because of the publication of the book, the guidelines (to conduct co-research with persons with disabilities). I think that is the result of good collaboration because of the published guidelines. For me, it shows the benefits of what we have done in the research. What we have done has been successful.

Irmansyah: The results of our research are used to create practical guidelines for co-researching with persons with disabilities. The existence of this published book, which is useful for people to read, and can be disseminated, is something that proves the involvement of persons with disabilities in this research collaboration. ... So, there is concrete evidence. ... And co-researchers with disabilities from the working group can claim that this is the result of our cooperation, the result of our partnership.

How did we grapple with and address ethical dilemmas?

The 'fighting spirit' to adapt with challenges

Irmansyah: Sometimes in the field, the conditions could be uncomfortable. ... It could be not so accessible and that's the reality. But we are fighters. For example, I got to an informant who lived in a place that required us to reach there through a footpath, and that was inaccessible for my wheelchair. On the one hand, that's the reality. On the other hand, we wanted to learn, we wanted to try to overcome the barrier. So, the challenges or barriers are common for us on a daily basis. We get used to the challenges ... so perhaps the dilemma is when I encountered situations that were quite uncomfortable, there was a concern that I would be seen as 'not trying hard enough', or 'not fighting enough'. ... This fighting spirit arose because I want to prove that despite our limitations as persons with disabilities, we can take actions as long as we are given the opportunity.

Back then, before I collaborated with NGOs [non-governmental organisations] and participated in community events, my own family and other non-disabled people perceived me as a person that couldn't do anything, that I just needed pity, and they had no thought of giving me a chance. I wasn't involved in my community because they saw that I have impairments. But since I wanted to learn and get along with the community, I grew my fighting spirit to prove them wrong. Eventually, my family and friends gave more opportunities and support which enabled me to act and participate.

Power imbalance due to daily allowance provision

Irmansyah: Perhaps we still cannot be fully open with ASB. On the positive side, ASB is open to criticism, so sometimes, we don't feel shy to tell or speak up when there is any dilemma. But we do something where we receive money to compensate for the transportation cost. So that's what I observe, some of us feel like it is better not to convey some concerns.

The inability to involve Persons with Disabilities in the analysis stage

Husna: I think we are so habituated with the idea that qualitative data analysis can only be done by using the 'commonly accepted' or 'legitimate' methods such as coding – which was complicated for co-researchers and would require an intense amount of time for them to learn how to do it. But I was wondering, who gets to decide what constitutes the 'legitimate' ways of analysing data? Is there any room for us to modify the standard qualitative methods while maintaining the validity and reliability of our analysis? From my standpoint, the non-disability researchers did not think of, nor explore, alternative ways that could allow co-researchers to participate in the analysis. Perhaps, if we dedicated more time and resources to devise a participatory method of analysing and interpreting the data, co-researchers would have a bigger opportunity to shape the knowledge we produced.

Takeaways for applying our approach

A partnership that is equal and suitable with the capacities of co-researchers with disabilities

Irmansyah: It is important to open and widen the collaboration with other stakeholders in the future, be it NGOs or governments. We need to improve the constant involvement of persons with disabilities.

Yassin: Support the Deaf community, so that we are more equal, and we can adapt. You should also adjust activities to the capacity of Deaf colleagues. You should understand their capacities, so they can work according to their potential. In presenting or interviewing informants using sign language, we should also show the writing and (illustrated) posters ... within the working group of persons with disabilities, there are different kinds of disabilities.

When you want to ask Deaf people to participate, provide a sign language interpreter and see if the ways of communicating are suitable. The previous training was not enough for me to conduct the research. We need a more sustainable collaboration, so your programme could be more inclusive, more solid and more equal.

Accessibility of information and research instruments

Irmansyah: There should be a collaboration or pairing with those who could translate and communicate in local languages to anticipate informants who cannot speak Indonesian at all, who only understand the local language. In the future, this should be taken into consideration.

Yassin: This is a suggestion for ASB and other NGOs: if you send any information, do not only distribute the information on the group chat on WhatsApp. Using private chat to inform us directly is better, so I can directly know what to prepare and what to do.

Full and meaningful participation

Irmansyah: Collaboration is really necessary ... it is a positive thing to improve the knowledge and empowerment of the groups who are still stigmatised, marginalised and discriminated against. So, if government agencies and academics implement programmes, they must not treat us as objects. If we are not involved, we will only be the object. But if we are involved, we can help the government's programmes. As for the NGOs, we can say that they already have the means and capacity, they just need to transfer them to persons with disabilities who have no capacity and skills yet. As for academics, this is the big role of academics, which is to disseminate, to share knowledge about, for example, the humanitarian issues, the importance of ensuring equality and promotion of human and disability rights.

Elias: My expectation for ASB, academia and government agencies, if they want to collaborate with persons with disabilities in the future, they should fully involve us, from planning until the final process. So we, as persons with disabilities or older persons, would have the courage to take responsibility when there are some questions from the local NGOs or any stakeholders who care about humanitarian actions … to give them tips and suggestions.

Zainab: We should be involved from the beginning until the end of the project. Not only at the beginning, or in the middle of the project. Everyone must be involved throughout the activities.

Husna: To achieve full participation in research collaboration, we cannot solely rely on a short-term project. For example, in a situation where co-researchers with disabilities have not been equipped with the knowledge and practical skills to design a research project, we need to transfer the knowledge first – which will require more dedicated time and resources outside of the project timeframe.

Reasonable accommodation, capacity building and decision-making in pairing the co-researcher teams

Irmansyah: Involve us in the decision-making even for simple things such as pairing co-researcher teams. For example, we could pair researchers with hearing difficulties with others with difficulties related to other functioning. During data collection, if there were unanticipated environmental barriers, we could support and assist each other. So, when pairing co-researchers in a team, we should consider the types

	of disabilities, for example, those with mobility or physical disabilities can be paired with those who do not have mobility difficulties.
Elias:	My expectation of other NGOs or water, sanitation and hygiene actors and government is, they should provide for the needs of the disability organisations, according to the needs of each functioning difficulty … involve us more, to hone our skills, capacity and knowledge about inclusive practices and other research topics. Also, there are still many local disability groups at district level which still have no umbrella organisations, they should be covered in the collaboration.

Enhancing the collaboration quality and visibility of partners with disabilities

Irmansyah:	ASB [and other organisations] could promote our collaboration more. For example, to show that there is disability participation, that the collaboration is inclusive … when Persons with Disabilities are involved, they will be able to participate.

Conclusion

In this chapter, we have presented how our different identities and lived experiences bring certain complexities in achieving full participation and equal collaborative partnerships among non-disability researchers and co-researchers with disabilities. The intersecting identities of non-disability researchers bring a certain privilege and contribute to the power imbalances that might affect co-researchers with disabilities. On the other hand, through our dialogue, we have also demonstrated how the preferences, needs and capacities of co-researchers are unique in the research collaboration because they have different lived experiences of vulnerability and discrimination. Further, sharing the same identity of persons with disabilities does not mean that co-researchers are homogeneous, as their disability identity intersects with a range of other identities, such as gender, socio-economic background, geographic location, culture and language. Acknowledging intersecting identities, privileges and vulnerabilities can determine appropriate and effective ways of implementing a research collaboration and shifting the power dynamics in favour of co-researchers with disabilities. Only then we can challenge the marginalisation of co-researchers with disabilities and work towards more inclusive participatory research processes.

Further reading

ASB Indonesia and the Philippines (2021a) *Investing in Inclusive Water, Sanitation and Hygiene (WASH): Lessons for Disability and Older Age Inclusion from the Central Sulawesi Response*, Yogyakarta: ASB Indonesia and the Philippines. Available from: https://www.asbindonesia.org/news-and-stories/investing-in-inclusive-water-sanitation-and-hygiene-wash-lessons-for-disability-and-older-age-inclusion-from-the-central-sulawesi-response-2/ [Accessed 22 November 2023].

ASB Indonesia and the Philippines (2021b) *Practical Guidelines for Co-researching with Persons with Disabilities: Reflections and Lessons Learned in Participatory Research on Inclusive WASH in Humanitarian Responses*, Yogyakarta: ASB Indonesia and the Philippines. Available from: https://www.elrha.org/researchdatabase/practical-guidelines-for-co-researching-with-people-with-disabilities/ [Accessed 22 November 2023].

Hernández-Saca, D.I., Gutmann Kahn, L. and Cannon, M.A. (2018) 'Intersectionality dis/ability research: How dis/ability research in education engages intersectionality to uncover the multidimensional construction of dis/abled experiences', *Review of Research in Education*, 42(1): 286–311.

Oliver, M. (1997) 'Emancipatory research: Realistic goal or impossible dream?', in C. Barnes and G. Mercer (eds) *Doing Disability Research*, Leeds: The Disability Press, pp 15–31.

References

Balcazar, F., Keys, C., Kaplan, D. and Suarez-Balcazar, Y. (2006) 'Participatory action research and people with disabilities: Principles and challenges', *Canadian Journal of Rehabilitation*, 12(2): 1–11.

Gartrell, A., Calgaro, E., Goddard, G. and Saorath, N. (2020) 'Disaster experiences of women with disabilities: Barriers and opportunities for disability inclusive disaster risk', *Global Environmental Change*, 64(102134): 1–11.

Kelman, I. and Stough, L.M. (2015) '(Dis) ability and (dis)aster', in I. Kelman and L.M. Stough (eds) *Disability and Disaster: Explorations and Exchanges*, London: Palgrave Macmillan, pp 3–14.

Kitchin, R. (2000) 'The researched opinions on research: Disabled people and disability research', *Disability & Society*, 15(1): 25–47.

Kusumowardoyo, C. and Wulansari, H. (2022) 'Towards meaningful participation in humanitarian studies: Co-researching with persons with disabilities in Central Sulawesi', *Disaster Prevention and Management*, 31(2): 158–165.

Oliver, M. (1992) 'Changing the social relations of research production?', *Disability, Handicap & Society*, 7(2): 101–114.

Ollerton, J. (2012) 'IPAR, an inclusive disability research methodology with accessible analytical tools', *International Practice Development Journal*, 2(3): 1–20.

Shakespeare, T. (2006) 'The social model of disability' in L.J. Davis (ed) *The Disability Studies Reader* (2nd edn), New York: Routledge, pp 197–204.

Stone, E. and Priestley, M. (1996) 'Parasites, pawns and partners: Disability research and the role of non-disabled researchers', *The British Journal of Sociology*, 47(4): 699–716.

Stough, L.M. and Kelman, I. (2018) 'People with disabilities and disasters', in H. Rodríguez, W. Donner and J.E. Trainor (eds) *Handbook of Disaster Research* (2nd edn), Cham: Springer, pp 243–262.

Twigg, J., Kett, M. and Lovell, E (2018) 'Disability inclusion and disaster risk reduction: Overcoming barriers to progress', *Briefing Note*. Available from: https://cdn.odi.org/media/documents/12324.pdf [Accessed 29 July 2022].

United Nations (2008) *Convention on the Rights of Persons with Disabilities: Article 1*. Available from: https://www.un.org/disabilities/documents/convention/convoptprot-e.pdf [Accessed 29 July 2022].

Zarb, G. (1992) 'On the road to Damascus: First steps towards changing the relations of disability research production', *Disability, Handicap & Society*, 7(2): 125–138.

PART III

Decolonising lived experience research

6

Ethical and decolonial considerations of co-research in refugee studies: what are we missing?

Atem Dau Atem and Maree Higgins

Key points

- This chapter disrupts the academy by redefining lived experience from a collective, community-led perspective.
- We use a collaborative writing process to generate new angles on the ethical conduct of collaborative research (co-research).
- We discuss two under-explored ethical dimensions of co-research in refugee studies: the ethics of relationship and the ethics of witnessing and documenting lived experiences.
- To ground our discussion, we describe our positionalities and critique our own research approaches.

Introduction

Co-research in refugee studies involves bearing witness to and documenting significant and ongoing marginalisation and oppression. Thus, it requires a deep commitment to, and a nuanced understanding of, relationships in research. On the surface, these statements will not surprise those involved in refugee research – they are common themes across the literature (see Ahmed, 2011; Kahn and Fábos, 2017). However, pervasive homogenising and colonising tendencies in refugee studies affects co-research, particularly influencing who can participate and how, as well as impacting the way the academy acknowledges and values contributions of co-researchers.

Our collaborative project on ethics in community-based participatory research (Atem et al, 2021) considered these and other challenges associated with co-research and identified two under-explored ethical insights about researching with people from refugee backgrounds. We name these *the ethics of relationship* and *the ethics of witnessing and documenting lived experiences*. Both have a significant bearing on the ethical conduct of collaborative research.

In this chapter, we explain what these ethics mean to us and what they could mean for refugee studies research, acknowledging the wisdom of our project group and honouring and building upon their work.

Who we are

Atem

I was born in South Sudan. My family left Sudan after the Second Civil War broke out in South Sudan. Like many South Sudanese, I found myself in Ethiopian refugee camps. Years later, hundreds of thousands of South Sudanese refugees were forced to flee back to South Sudan as the Ethiopian rebels liberated Ethiopia. As violence escalated in South Sudan, South Sudanese who had just come back to South Sudan from Ethiopia joined many more South Sudanese displaced persons to find their way to Kenya. This happened to my family, and we arrived in Kakuma Refugee Camp in 1993. In 2002, I came to Australia through its Humanitarian Program as a refugee like most members who make up my South Sudanese Australian community. I attended the University of Canberra and then the Australian National University where I completed a PhD on the settlement experiences of South Sudanese humanitarian entrants in Western Sydney. The thesis explores settlement from the perspectives of South Sudanese humanitarian entrants themselves (Atem, 2022).

Maree

As stated in Chapter 1, I am a white, cisgender, heterosexual woman born in Australia of Irish heritage, who grew up in Sydney, Australia, on land that is now recognised as unceded Bedegal land. I had the privilege of completing a social work degree and gaining international work experience in my 20s. Living and working in a rural community in South Africa for two years, I provided career advice and counselling to young people experiencing the everyday challenges of adolescence as well as sexual assault, grief and loss, ill health, and social isolation. Through the mentoring of Aunties within the school community I became conversant in two of the local languages, which helped me tailor my work to the needs of the school community. I was often told (and also felt) that 'Mother Africa' looked after me. Returning to Sydney, I sought ways to reciprocate the care I received, and became an advocate for refugee rights, initially providing support services for refugee applicants, and then in education and research roles. My doctoral thesis, 'Like gold scattered in the sand' (Higgins, 2019), explored understandings and constructions of human rights from the perspectives of African families from refugee backgrounds. My research continues to focus on human rights of people from refugee backgrounds.

Our projects

We met in 2019. Atem, who was working as a community development officer, planned to conduct community-based research and reached out to Maree to collaborate on the project. The funding priorities of Atem's workplace changed, so things did not proceed as planned. Soon after, with the help of some funding from her workplace, Maree invited Atem to collaborate on the three co-design projects we discuss in this section.

Our first co-designed project explored best-practice ethical processes in community-based participatory research in refugee studies (Atem et al, 2021). Co-researchers were from Syria, Bosnia, South Sudan, Vietnam, Afghanistan, Mauritius, the United Kingdom, the United States and Australia. We gathered at local sites in 2019 and shared food, conversations and insights about co-research. Following these initial meetings, we developed a critique of current ethical guidelines for refugee research, highlighting eight ethical concerns, and articulating ten principles of ethical practice, which all project members authored (Atem et al, 2021). One important observation from this project is that the term 'co-researcher' often excludes by distinguishing between 'researchers' and 'co-researchers' (Atem et al, 2021: 3). In our writing, we use terms to break down such (un)intended binary representations.

Our second collaborative project explored African ways of knowing, being and doing human rights. We designed a workshop for the 2019 African Studies of Australasia and the Pacific conference in Dunedin, Aotearoa New Zealand, where participants shared stories, songs, sayings and poems that conveyed family and community understandings of human rights.

This chapter is our third collaborative project. To co-write this chapter, we created a dialogical space, informed by Homi Bhabha's *third space* (2012: 55), gathering regularly for more than a year to reflect on our experiences of co-research through our respective cultural lenses. Bhabha describes the third space as 'contradictory and ambivalent ... [in which] cultural signs can be appropriated, translated, rehistoricised, and read anew' (Bhabha, 2012: 55). In these discussions, we focused on 'ah-ha!' moments in our co-research, times when *mis*understandings led to *new* understandings between us. We shared stories about research experiences that had resulted in uncertainty or messiness (or both) and explored the implications of these experiences together. Lenette (2020) argues that co-research involves more uncertainty and messiness than academics tend to reveal in their writing. For us, reflecting on uncertainty and messiness was valuable as it emphasised the disproportionate influence of western models of research virtue in our work, and we surface these elements as we tease out the meanings of the 'ethics of relationship' and the 'ethics of witnessing and documenting lived experiences' discussed in this chapter.

Our discussion of the ethics of relationship and the ethics of witnessing and documenting lived experiences sits within a broader decolonial discourse gaining momentum in refugee studies (Reimer et al, 2019; Lenette, 2022a). Decolonial discourse highlights the persistent silencing and absence of diverse worldviews in much of the literature drawn upon in the social sciences (Dunford, 2017) and emphasises that no one person can assume to know all that can be known about human realities (Maldonado-Torres, 2011). Along with critiquing co-research literature, we provide vignettes to illustrate our collaborative meaning making. In the vignettes we share in this chapter, we write about how our dialogues have enabled us to *rethink* established rules and assumptions about co-research. We end with implications for refugee studies researchers.

Critique of co-research literature

Our review of the literature on ethics in co-research with people from refugee backgrounds for our first project revealed serious limitations in the sector. While conceptual articles often describe relevant high-level ethical issues and research strategies (for example, Gibbes and Skop, 2020), empirical studies generally provide very little commentary about ethical issues that arise, and limited discussion of potentially diverse expectations and agendas in co-research, although there are some heartening exceptions (for example, McSweeney et al, 2021). Explicit discussion of decolonisation is missing in refugee-studies literature, with few exceptions (an example is Reimer et al, 2019). Moreover, much of the literature is 'sanitised', robbing refugee studies scholars of opportunities to examine and strengthen their practices, discuss uncertainties that arise, and reflect upon mistakes that occur (Lenette, 2020). The absence of formal guidelines for co-research with people from refugee backgrounds exacerbates this situation.

There appears to be limited co-authorship with people from refugee backgrounds in the refugee studies literature which perpetuates epistemic injustice (see Chapter 1). First-hand accounts of lived experiences are most often included in mediated form, with tenured academics and research students deciding what and how refugee lived experiences are presented and exerting significant control over meaning-making and analysis. According to decolonial scholarship, this is highly problematic as it can render certain experiences invisible and universalise experience (Maldonado-Torres, 2011; Dunford, 2017; Amelina, 2022). Our research suggests that, when presented second-hand, lived experience generally illustrates hardship, trauma and struggle. Experiences are often decontextualised and at risk of reinforcing university-based researchers' or funders' agendas, rather than reflecting the concerns of people from refugee backgrounds.

When narratives of struggle lack critical engagement with underlying structural explanations, a vulnerability discourse is perpetuated, and paternalistic, patronising and potentially coercive stances in co-research are permitted. In such contexts, there is little room for alternate narratives, and what matters most to people is readily obscured. Thus, power and representation should be considered when documenting and disseminating knowledge about people from refugee backgrounds (Atem et al, 2021; Higgins et al, 2023). Lived experience authorship in scholarly literature can complement other strategies, such as co-presenting in diverse fora, that honour lived experience-led scholarship at the knowledge dissemination stage (Lenette, 2022b). However, including people from refugee backgrounds as lead authors on scholarly papers is no guarantee that one's work will challenge western norms or be imbued with decolonial values. Such decisions must be accompanied by critical reflexivity and open, honest communication. As in other stages of research, writers must remain alert to how dominant narratives can be (re)produced.

Student et al (2017) provide an example of this careful and reflexive decision-making in a lived experience-led film and writing project. A student from a refugee background, R Student is the sole protagonist and lead author of a film and publication which centre their subjective experiences of resilience, perseverance and discrimination in higher education. While exemplary in that each author describes their positionality, R Student remains anonymous; they choose a pseudonym and have their image blurred on camera due to fears for family members in their country of origin (Student et al, 2017: 581).

We use a co-authorship model in several articles and book chapters to centre lived experiences of people from refugee backgrounds with disability (Wells et al, 2020; Dew et al, 2021; Higgins et al, 2023; Murad et al, 2023). These articles critique and inform disability services and exemplify the agency of people from refugee backgrounds with disability in policy making. Although these publications include continuous and inclusive dialogue, co-author checking and translation of material, and advocacy for the material to be published in a community language as well as the colonial language, norms which we are at the forefront of introducing into the field, we do not elaborate on our careful and inclusive processes, and do not consistently describe our positionalities, indicating we have further to go in our efforts.

We are learning through reflection about the impact of the silences and absences in such work. Using four vignettes, we now share some of these learnings.

Vignette one – Atem: limitations of western research norms

During fieldwork for my PhD, I presented my research to a Dinka-speaking audience. I wanted South Sudanese living in Sydney to participate in my research, and as a Dinka speaker, I assumed that I could effectively communicate what I was doing and persuade people to volunteer to be interviewed. I also wanted people to know that, when they saw me at future events or community activities, I was not just a mere participant, but was collecting information for my thesis.

That day, I was on my feet looking at a full community hall, about a hundred people, with faces filled with anticipation. People were curious. Many of those men, women and young people knew me – either through family, my work in the community, or hearing about me from others, as you do in the South Sudanese community. That is how that community works – everyone knows everyone else in some way.

I introduced myself and thanked people for the opportunity to talk with them. I then turned to the subject matter of my research. I suddenly stopped. For the listener, my pause heightened the anticipation. I could feel the tension building in the audience. I could feel it rising in myself. I realised I was not sure how to explain my studies, thesis, research, methodology, data collection and analysis. I was not sure how to tell people that I was about to collect information from them and turn it into something that is attributed to ME forever. I could not find the words. In the Dinka culture, no one writes a thesis to become a subject matter expert. No one does formal research to gain knowledge and understanding of the social world. This does not mean there is no expertise. The community often recognises individuals for their expertise, for example, the rainmaker who can predict the weather, the healer who is the village doctor, the spear master who mediates conflict, and the wise counsel of Elders who adjudicate on all matters of the law, to name but a few.

In this situation, I struggled to explain my purpose. The audience was getting anxious and agitated. They were not sure what I was talking about. I was getting frustrated by my poor communication mainly due to my inability to recall suitable words in Dinka that could effectively communicate what I had in mind. I was acutely aware that some words associated with data collection, such as *research interview*, may trigger people. The word for interview is the same word the police or security agencies use for interrogation. It is also associated with the stressful interview process that people must undergo to justify why they should be offered resettlement places, with immigration lawyers looking for inconsistencies in the narratives. These interviews are often traumatic.

I went away from this event feeling very disappointed with myself. My discomfort resonated throughout the recruitment phase: because of my dissatisfaction and uncertainty, I invited only those South Sudanese who had completed or were at university, worked in professional roles and spoke English well. Therefore, most of my research participants were not your typical South Sudanese – they were educated, held professional jobs and spoke high-level English. Reflecting on this challenge left me dissatisfied with the norms in refugee research practice, especially the western notion of informed consent, which assumes an understanding of research practices and research culture underpinned by western notions of knowledge creation and intellectual property. Applying these assumptions to the refugee context may result in great harm.

Western research paradigms significantly downplay diverse knowledges and obscure knowledge grounded in everyday lived experiences. Reflecting on this with Maree, I explained that from my Dinka perspective, reality is about the *lived experience* of the world around us and has two aspects. First, this world is both a physical and a metaphysical world (explained later). Second, reality is *social*, that is, lived experience has to be experienced collectively for it to make sense. An individual's private experience of the world has little currency; the community as a collective makes sense of lived experience. Each person injects their individualised lived experiences into the communal discourse, and the community interprets lived experiences collectively. The wisdom gained from such processes determines what reality is. The collective process of learning about reality is underpinned by communal values, morals and ethical principles that were not obvious even to community members engaged in that process. Reality understood in this way must have a place and function in the social, physical and metaphysical world. Lived experience that cannot be placed and therefore has no function does not quite constitute reality and is of no interest.

Here is an example to explain the physical and metaphysical forms of our world, as mentioned earlier:

- Touching a tree – experience.
- The social significance of touching a tree – a ceremonial act.
- The tree as a manifestation of something superhuman.

Experiencing the tree through touch is not enough to realise the reality of the tree. Touching the tree brings it to the awareness of the community around it. The experience of the tree is a small part of reality. It does not explain how the tree ended up there and its place and function in the social and spiritual life of the community. The tree is known and understood through its relationship to the *social*. The question then is: *what is the role of the tree in enhancing or diminishing the communal life?* The tree provides shade. The shade provides shelter from the sun. People sit under the tree during the hottest part of the day to carry on their social and spiritual life. The tree enables social life. Community members talk about and look forward to meeting under the tree to perform rituals. They name the tree in songs. Community members tell stories about the tree, which becomes part of the community psyche and community living. The tree is a gift from the gods. It is now real.

So, in my culture, reality is about the relationship between *lived experiences* and their social and metaphysical functions in the community. Upon reflection, if I could go back to my past self and give him advice, it would be to workshop my approach with key knowledge holders in the community to better centre the distinctive perspectives on the reality of my Dinka collaborators, rather than relying on the guidance of my western supervisors. This would have empowered diverse members of the Dinka community to participate as equal research partners.

Vignette two – Maree: probing beyond someone's boundaries

During my doctoral fieldwork in Sydney, I met with someone who had prepared a written statement for our interview. As we began to discuss human rights, they unfolded several closely written pages of text and began to orate their beautifully crafted essay on human rights. I was humbled by their preparation for our discussion and transfixed as they shared their perspectives on human rights with me. I remember feeling grateful to have permission to audio-record their words; this allowed me to remain in the moment and note small aspects of their demeanour and emphasis along the way. I nodded throughout, acknowledging each of their statements encouragingly.

Once they finished, I reflected on what I had heard and identified that a question was swirling in me: how did they personally feel about human rights, and what stories and experiences could they share to illustrate this? I was, after all, researching lived experiences of human rights and I had an ethics committee–approved semi-structured interview guide that prompted me to ask such questions to gain a nuanced understanding of this topic and compare different perspectives. I wondered what to do. Should I thank this person for their contributions and conclude the interview? Or should I invite them to provide a personal perspective on the material they had presented? I decided to tentatively invite this person to share something more personal about human rights, and they obliged. We sat together for quite some time as they shared stories of heartache, fear, exclusion, ill-treatment and dehumanisation in resettlement. Each story was rich in detail and highly relevant to my study. I listened, documented and bore witness to their stories of suffering.

When the transcript of our interview was ready, I shared it with this person, asking them to check it and advise of any changes or aspects they wished to remove or change. Their response was brief: they wished to withdraw entirely from the research. Their response provided no explanation. I wrote to them, assuring them that their wishes would be respected, gratefully acknowledging their contributions, apologising for any misstep on my part, and seeking their guidance on what I could have done differently. I received no response. Guided by my supervisors, I reported the situation to the research ethics committee and removed this person's stories from my analysis. This person's reality, and the potential harms caused, have stayed with me, though.

Reflecting on this experience with Atem, I learned more about the ethics of relationship and the ethics of witnessing and documenting. While it is hard to know for sure, it seems that this person had set boundaries with me by bringing their written contributions to the interview, and that my decision to probe beyond this boundary altered our relationship by privileging my agenda over theirs. I also reflected on my role as a *witness*; what did this person want me to bear witness to and how did my conduct reflect other oppressive stances this person has endured? Drawing on the work of Oliver (2001), Atem reminded me that witnessing and documenting refugee experience in co-research must be dialogic, because torture, trauma and oppression can affect one's inner dialogue, as we discuss later. Early on, I regretted that I chose this path, but in dialogue with Atem, I came to understand what I had done in a new way. I may have done what was *ethically permitted*, but not what was *relationally right*. If I could go back to my past research self and give her advice, it would be to *prioritise relationships over gathering data*.

Vignette three – Atem: honouring lived experience

During my doctoral fieldwork in Sydney, two women from refugee backgrounds requested to participate in my research. They appeared very eager for me to record their stories. I was reluctant because I was worried about their expectations of me as a researcher and their ability to give informed consent, but these two women were adamant they wanted their stories recorded. I had been trained to explain that I had no capacity to advocate on their behalf in my role as a researcher, so I agreed to meet them but made sure they clearly understood these limitations. In reply, the women explained that they felt that no one was listening to them. By recording their stories, I offered them the chance to be heard in the context of my research, and possibly by others in the future.

One of the women had her twin babies removed from her care as soon as they were born because of her husband's drinking and rowdy behaviour, which caught the attention of neighbours, who reported concerns about her welfare to the authorities. This woman felt that authorities punished her and her twins even though they did nothing wrong.

The second woman's husband was fatally assaulted when he protested the racial harassment he experienced. The authorities investigated the murder, but no one was brought to justice. This woman did everything in her power to persuade the authorities to bring the culprit to justice, but they were reluctant to act. As I listened to her story, she emphasised her strong feelings about this injustice and the failure of the authorities to address it.

What purpose did listening serve in this research? Should I have agreed to witness the stories of these two women, when I felt I could do so little to advocate for them? Western ethical norms emphasise the importance of beneficence, non-maleficence, informed consent and voluntary participation. Yet, these norms do not address the micro-ethics of research, that is, ethics that occurs 'in everyday practice: the micro-dynamics and power fluctuations that can occur within groups and communities and among researchers; the everyday and interpersonal risks and benefits of research' (Atem et al, 2021: 4). Reflecting on my assumptions with Maree, I realised that I was uncomfortable about my role due to western constructions of research as neutral and objective, and due to age and gender norms in my Dinka community. Looking back, for the two women, I feel that witnessing and documenting their stories was about restoring their agency by challenging authorities who had failed them. My act of recording the women's stories enabled them to take back the power they vested in those authorities, even though I didn't take further steps to advocate for a better outcome. Their research involvement brought to light structural and systematic injustices that were previously hidden: denied lived experiences became undeniable.

These vignettes unsettle both of our assumptions about research relationships. Acutely aware of the disconnects between western and South Sudanese worldviews and the limits of his power to advocate for immediate and just outcomes, Atem connects the experience of being consulted and heard with the experience of justice. Noting a disconnect between her role as a witness and her role as interviewer based on an approved research agenda, Maree reassesses her embodiment of humanness and care in fieldwork.

These stories also raise questions for us about informed consent in social justice research. If informed consent provides permission to researchers, what does this permission represent? Does it affirm that the researcher can use someone's story to illustrate an insight, a trend, a set of circumstances? What of the western practice of aggregating and disaggregating knowledge shared, drawing themes from stories in a way that all but removes the person from the original data and makes them the researcher's property? If this aspect of research, which is fundamental to ethical research guidelines, remains a procedural activity, it is expressly designed to support the research agenda rather than relationships, which is problematic. Micro-ethics, where issues that might be perceived as unimportant 'come to matter in ethical ways' (Mathias, 2020: 253), can help to address everyday aspects of power and relationships. This can prompt greater mindfulness about what and how witnessing occurs and can unsettle the unilateral application of informed consent, enabling it to be re-envisioned as an invitation to witness. For example, in Maree's case, rather than asking, 'Do you consent to participate in this project?', Maree would ask the person, 'What about your experiences are you willing for me to witness?'.

Vignette four – Atem and Maree: flexible collaboration

Our co-facilitated human rights workshop at the African Studies Conference in Aotearoa New Zealand in 2019 is an example of us collaborating and doing things differently. We co-wrote the abstract and co-developed the workshop plan, prioritising collaboration throughout the design process. We remember re-writing the plan in a Dunedin café while the staff closed down for the night around us! We had been discussing ways to cultivate participant safety, discovery and agency in relation to human rights and had several last-minute ideas to incorporate. On the day of the workshop, we had about 11 participants, eight from African backgrounds, and three from Anglo- or European backgrounds. Equal numbers of men and women participated in the discussion.

We introduced ourselves, explained our purpose and approach, and emphasised our interest in diverse perspectives. As we did so, several African-background participants expressed interest in the topic but stated that they did not feel comfortable with the room setup. The chairs were arranged in long rows, like an exam hall or a lecture theatre, and participants wanted a setup that could facilitate free and flowing dialogue. We invited the group to move the chairs into a better configuration. Very quickly, the chairs were rearranged into a circle. Now, each participant could see one another. This seating arrangement is commonly known in African contexts as the learning circle, used to discuss complex problems and brainstorm solutions. The learning circle emphasises equality and enables people with different abilities and capacities to discuss issues and solutions as equal to that moment. When we reflected on what had happened, we were struck by the symbolism of the choice to form a learning circle and the way re-formulating the physical layout re-oriented the research relationships. The learning circle challenged the academic hierarchy we had inadvertently reinforced when we entered the room and initiated the workshop without first considering the room layout.

Academic hierarchies reinforce the notion of expertise as a function of empirical knowledge rather than lived experience: a single individual will usually take a prominent position in relation to participants, for example, standing in front of a learning group and directing the discussion. When we invited participants to help problem-solve this issue, we supported their sense of ownership over the process, and our workshop became a lively discussion where participants described many fables, sayings and stories that shed light on human rights ideals.

One participant became very animated and shared about a similar project he had worked on many years prior, for a global organisation, that had created a repository of similar knowledge, which had over time become defunct. He offered to share this with us and expressed the hope that our dialogue might re-enliven this engagement with African perspectives on human rights.

Many participants indicated their interest in an ongoing collaboration to extend the lexicon of human rights and write up our findings for publication.

Reflections on our experiences

Having reflected on how western research paradigms mis/shape co-researcher relationships, we discuss the implications for co-research in refugee studies.

The ethics of relationship

Existing discussions of co-research relationships emphasise dialogue, doing no harm and not stealing people's stories (for example, Pittaway et al, 2010). As demonstrated by our reflexive narratives, the *ethics of relationship* takes us beyond these moral principles and guidelines, towards cultural safety where researchers from the academy exercise continuous reflexivity about their ways of being in the world, their agendas and their impact on others, and pay close attention to lived experience co-researchers' perspectives on the research throughout (Lenette et al, 2020).

For us, the ethics of relationship centres the worldviews of co-researchers from refugee backgrounds, and (re-)affirms their expertise. In this model, co-research is 'more than a job': researchers from the academy must be flexible and vulnerable as core responsibilities of the research. Relationships that are based on genuine respect, honesty, openness and transparency enable the dynamic exploration of challenging (ethical) issues that arise in co-research. As Atem's reflections show, they also crystallise what matters most to refugee communities, posing questions of clear social and metaphysical value.

The ethics of witnessing and documenting

Esther Mujawayo, a survivor of the Rwandan genocide, describes bearing witness as dialogic, that is, 'a social space, within which survivors can negotiate, and eventually reclaim, the meaning of their survival and assert the demands of the traumatic aftermath they face' (translated by Dauge-Roth, 2009: 166). Similarly, Oliver describes witnessing as a space in which survivors can 'perform … what one knows from firsthand experiences [as well as] what is beyond knowledge or recognition' (Oliver, 2001: 86). Indeed, both authors describe the tensions between what one knows (or can know) from first-hand experience, and what they feel and remember but cannot verify or clearly account for.

Drawing on these ideas, for us, *the ethics of witnessing and documenting* is upholding survivor agency and enabling truly collaborative meaning-making through reflexive dialogue. Because oppression can destroy people's experience of their own inner dialogue (Oliver, 2001), the ethics of witnessing and documenting goes beyond informed consent to promote the 'repair of the inner witness', enabling the reassertion of co-researchers from refugee background's 'subjective agency and humanity' (Oliver, 2001: 92–93). Thus, the ethics of witnessing and documenting (re)turns power to those with refugee lived experience in the elaboration of their stories and regarding how their stories are interpreted and shared. As we highlight in this chapter, this is important not just for individuals who have experienced refugee traumas but for the collective – all those responsible for considering the place and function of such experiences in the social and spiritual life of the community.

Ways forward

Given what is currently missing in refugee studies co-research, we see two important ways forward for those who aim to disrupt colonial research practices.

The first way forward relates to *the ethics of relationship*. Steps are required at the micro, meso and macro level to constructively (re)centre the worldviews of people from refugee backgrounds in refugee studies co-research. For example, ethical guidelines and protocols are required to establish the standards for ethically permissible *and* relationally right research practices. Within these frameworks, tenured academics must attune themselves to micro-dynamics and power fluctuations so often ignored in refugee studies, through practices that are reflexive, human and accountable to individuals and communities from refugee backgrounds. In support of such practices, institutions and publishing houses must problematise sanitised accounts of lived experience research and elevate approaches that cede power and engage creatively and meaningfully with ambivalence and uncertainty.

The second way forward relates to *the ethics of witnessing and documenting*. It should no longer be acceptable to provide mediated accounts of lived experience in the academy. New processes and strategies need to take the place of old approaches, a situation that implicates academic research training as well as business-as-usual research. Where knowledge development is led by lived experience, strategies that uphold survivor agency and support collaborative meaning-making are required, including naming people with lived experiences as leads on grants and publications, and attending to epistemic justice during research design, implementation, analysis, dissemination and evaluation.

Further reading

Carpi, E. and Owusu, P. (2022) 'Slavery, lived realities, and the decolonisation of forced migration histories: An interview with Dr Portia Owusu', *Migration Studies*, 10(1): 87–93.

Hearn, F., Biggs, L., Brown, S., Tran, L., Shwe, S., Noe, T.M.P., Toke, S., Alqas Alias, M., Essa, M., Hydari, S., Szwarc, J. and Riggs, E. (2022) 'Having a say in research directions: The role of community researchers in participatory research with communities of refugee and migrant background', *International Journal of Environmental Research and Public Health*, 19(4844): 1–14.

Qi, J., Manathunga, C., Singh M. and Bunda, T. (2021) 'Transcultural and First Nations doctoral education and epistemological border-crossing: Histories and epistemic justice', *Teaching in Higher Education*, 26(3): 340–353.

Singh, N., Lokot, M., Undie, C-C., Onyango, M.A., Morgan, R., Harmer, A., Freedman, J. and Heidari, S. (2021) 'Research in forced displacement: Guidance for a feminist and decolonial approach', *The Lancet*, 397(10274): 560–562.

References

Ahmed, S. (2011) 'Father of no one's son', *Third Text*, 25(3): 325–334.

Amelina, A. (2022) 'Knowledge production for whom? Doing migrations, colonialities and standpoints in non-hegemonic migration research', *Ethnic and Racial Studies*, 45(13): 2393–2415.

Atem, A.D. (2022) 'In the search for the good life: Settlement experiences of South Sudanese families in Western Sydney', PhD thesis, Canberra, Australian National University.

Atem, A.D., Bajraktarevic-Hayward, J., Nguyen, D., Al Kalmashi, R., Hanna, B., Higgins, M., Lenette, C., Milne, E.J., Nunn, C. and Gardner, J. (2021) *Ethics and Community-based Participatory Research with People from Refugee Backgrounds*, Kensington: UNSW, STARTTS, Coventry University and Manchester Metropolitan University.

Bhabha, H.K. (2012) *The Location of Culture*, 2nd edn, Hoboken: Taylor and Francis.

Dauge-Roth, A. (2009) 'Testimonial encounter: Esther Mujawayo's dialogic art of witnessing', *French Cultural Studies*, 20(2): 165–180.

Dew, A., Lenette, C., Smith, L., Boydell, K., Bibby, H., Lappin, J., Coello, M., Raman, S., Velkou, K., Wells, R., Momartin, S., Blunden, H., Higgins, M., Murad, M., Barry, J. and Mohammad, Y. (2021) '"To the Arabic community disability is not normal": Multiple stakeholder perceptions of the understandings of disability among Iraqi and Syrian people from refugee backgrounds', *Journal of Refugee Studies*, 34(3): 2849–2870.

Dunford, R. (2017) 'Toward a decolonial global ethics', *Journal of Global Ethics*, 13(3): 380–397.

Gibbes, C. and Skop, E. (2020) 'The messiness of co-produced research with gatekeepers of resettled refugee communities', *Journal of Cultural Geography*, 37(3): 278–295.

Higgins, M. (2019) 'Like gold scattered in the sand: Human rights understandings and constructions from the perspective of African families from refugee backgrounds', PhD thesis, North Sydney, Australian Catholic University.

Higgins, M., Murad, M., Robinson, K., Dew, A., Boydell, K., McKay, F., Watson, J., Coello, M., Smith, L., Johnson, K. and Wells, R. (2023) 'Engaged advocacy: A framework for inclusion of people from refugee and asylum-seeking backgrounds in disability policy', in S. Robinson and K.R. Fisher (eds) *Research Handbook on Disability Policy*, Cheltenham: Edward Elgar, pp 305–321.

Kahn, L. and Fábos, A.H. (2017) 'Witnessing and disrupting: The ethics of working with testimony for refugee advocacy', *Journal of Human Rights Practice*, 9(3): 526–533.

Lenette, C. (2020) 'Sitting with the mess', in P. Wadds, N. Apoifis, S. Schmeidl and K. Spurway (eds) *Navigating Fieldwork in the Social Sciences*, Cham: Palgrave Macmillan, pp 39–60.

Lenette, C. (2022a) *Participatory Action Research: Ethics and Decolonization*, New York: Oxford University Press.

Lenette, C. (2022b) 'Cultural safety in participatory arts-based research: How can we do better?', *Journal of Participatory Research Methods*, 3(1): 1–15.

Lenette, C., Bordbar, A., Hazara, A., Lang, E. and Yahya, S. (2020) '"We were not merely participating; we were leading the discussions": Participation and self-representation of refugee young people in international advocacy', *Journal of Immigrant and Refugee Studies*, 18(4): 390–404.

Maldonado-Torres, N. (2011) 'Thinking through the decolonial turn: Post-continental interventions in theory, philosophy, and critique – an introduction', *Tansmodernity: Journal of Peripheral Cultural Production of the Luso-Hispanic World*, 1(2): 1–15.

Mathias, J. (2020) 'Sticky ethics: Environmental activism and the limits of ethical freedom in Kerala, India', *Anthropological Theory*, 20(3): 253–276.

McSweeney, M., Hakiza, R. and Namukhula, J. (2021) 'Participatory action research and visual and digital methods with refugees in Kampala, Uganda: Process, ethical complexities, and reciprocity', *Sport in Society*, 25(3): 485–505.

Murad, M., assisted by Salameh, M. and Higgins, M., translated by Salemah, M. (2023) 'My work advocating for the Syrian community', in S. Robinson and K.R. Fisher (eds) *Research Handbook on Disability Policy*, Cheltenham: Edward Elgar, pp 322–329.

Oliver, K. (2001) *Witnessing: Beyond Recognition*, Minneapolis: University of Minnesota Press.

Pittaway, E., Bartolomei, L. and Hugman, R. (2010) '"Stop stealing our stories": The ethics of research with vulnerable groups', *Journal of Human Rights Practice*, 2(2): 229–251.

Reimer, K., Kaukko, M., Dunwoodie, K., Wilkinson, J. and Webb, S. (2019) 'Acknowledging the head, heart, hands and feet: Research with refugees and people seeking asylum in higher education', *Widening Participation and Lifelong Learning*, 21(2): 190–208.

Student, R., Kendall, K. and Day, L. (2017) 'Being a refugee university student: A collaborative auto-ethnography', *Journal of Refugee Studies*, 30(4): 580–604.

Wells, R., Murad, M., Higgins, M., Smith, L., Lenette, C., Lappin, J., Dew, A., Boydell, K., Bibby, H., Cassaniti, M., Isaacs, D., Raman, S. and Zwi, K. (2020) 'Exploring the intersection of human rights, health, disability and refugee status: An arts-based approach', *Australian Journal of Human Rights*, 26(3): 387–404.

7

Combating colonially pathologised universalisation: a transwoman's Indo-Australian lived experience

Estelle Keerthana Ramaswamy

Key points

- This chapter disrupts the academy by challenging western conceptualisations of gender diversity that dominate knowledge production about trans and gender diverse people.
- These privileged views are imposed widely as globally relevant, while knowledge from majority-world countries such as India is subsumed and categorised as indigenous to a specific place and time. Trans and gender diverse researchers' representation might only be on the rise in western countries.
- Research on trans and gender diverse people has largely been framed by cisgendered people, and this has often led to pathologising us and our lived experiences.
- Trans and gender diverse people include a wide array of people with different everyday struggles, which are often misconstrued as universal.
- Research and policy making at all stages must include trans and gender diverse people using ethical models of participation.

Introduction

Many might find it rather difficult to remember what happened when they were children aged five or six, except if those instances were of profound significance. Trans and gender diverse persons, especially transwomen, might agree with my claim that they could never forget the moment in their lives when they felt and experienced a realisation of some 'peculiarity' with who they were. For many trans souls, this realisation could occur at any age during childhood or even after adolescence. These realisations, irrespective of age, are all valid and warrant respect and consideration.

Some people, including people from transgender communities, might term their realisations as a 'change' they encountered. Consequently, horrendous questions follow: 'At what age did you change?', instead of focusing on the realisation(s). With these horrendous questions comes the stereotype that trans people must be a particular way to be accepted as trans people among mainstream communities and for any government welfare measures to apply.[1] This stereotyping reverberates in many policies. For example, in India, the Transgender Persons (Protection of Rights) Act (2019) has this clear goal. It is particularly heartbreaking that the Act, which is meant to improve the lives of transgender people, makes their lives even more difficult under the guise of weeding out people who might claim welfare schemes illegally.

In the Indian context, transwomen find it very difficult to welcome, accept and support other transwomen without a hidden agenda of talking new transwomen into transitioning completely. I explain this in detail in my recollections which come later. Transwomen in India hold many stereotypes. For example, many only accept transwomen who have their own long hair. Many transwomen favour the word 'change' over 'realisation'.

In this chapter, I, Estelle Keerthana (pronouns she/they), share my lived experiences as a transwoman,[2] a non-binary person and a Thirunangai (Tamil equivalent to the western concept of transwoman) from Chennai, Tamil Nadu, India, and my journey and experiences in Australia. I share my views on ethics in research that involves trans and gender diverse people.

Methodology

This chapter is an autoethnographic account of my life and lived experiences. Autoethnography is a qualitative research methodology which demonstrates how one knows, names and interprets one's personal and cultural lived experiences in artistic and analytical ways (Holman Jones et al, 2015). In other words, autoethnography provides a description of and critiques culturally valued beliefs and practices by employing a researcher's personal experiences as a lens. This means that autoethnographic research focuses on a researcher and their relationship with the world.

In addition to focusing on the researcher and their relationship with the world, autoethnography is a decolonised research methodology (Williams, 2021; Zaharin and Pallotta-Chiarolli, 2022). Western research methodologies do not usually involve researchers who belong to marginalised communities, but those who distance themselves from the study subject, and often impose their beliefs (Williams, 2021). Further, western research methodologies are often transactional wherein researchers might visit a community to conduct their research and communities often do not hear back from them. Hence, autoethnography is best suited for this chapter as it is a decolonised research methodology.

Using autoethnography may attract criticism. One such criticism may be about the autobiographical element of autoethnography. However, beyond being just autobiographical, autoethnography analyses the wider social and cultural environments (Wiesner, 2018). Autoethnography can help uncover the complicated and emotionally laden positionality of a transgender and non-binary person by using reflexivity as a tool for research (Wiesner, 2018). In addition, autoethnography ensures rigour and quality in qualitative research (Koopman et al, 2020). Therefore, autoethnography is the best-suited research methodology to understand decolonised lived experiences and disrupt and transform knowledge.

Positionality

To make sense of one's lived experiences, it is essential to elaborate on and understand positionality(ies), that is, someone's particular philosophical stance in relation to other perspectives that might underpin their approach (Hopkins et al, 2016). Authors should declare their positionality in their research and writing to facilitate readers' understanding as to why an author posits certain opinions in a certain way. In other words, there is transparency in how researchers' positionalities might impact their work (Secules et al, 2021). Stating positionalities establishes the authors' own motivations for their research, their worldviews and beliefs, and the components which embody their research process.

Positionalities also help in identifying researchers' bias(es) which may in turn help gain new insights about the research project, its processes, and participants' identities. As such, each person might have multiple overlapping identities through which they derive various meanings (Bourke, 2014). To facilitate readers' engagement with my points, I first present my positionalities, which also helps in understanding the significance and the timeliness of this chapter.

I categorise myself as a transwoman/transfemme person and Thirunangai. I am the third child born to parents who are largely self-made. I was born and raised in the southeast-Indian metropolitan city of Chennai (formerly Madras). I experienced all my upbringing and school education in an urban centre and in English. I then had a brief stint in Australia as an international student before returning to India to pursue a bachelor's degree in psychology. I worked and ran a business for a few years before embarking on a master's degree to progress to a PhD. I have a master's in development policy and practice and at the time of writing, I am pursuing a PhD in Australia. I am the first Tamil-Indian transwoman/transfemme person and Thirunangai to receive a scholarship to pursue a PhD at an Australian university.

Each of the categories I discuss has shaped my lived experiences. These experiences have helped me become competitive and well-versed in English, have helped me find opportunities outside my country, and have opened up worldviews and beliefs that may not necessarily be those of many other authors from the same background. I first recount my lived experiences, from the beginning of my life in India up until now when I am working towards a PhD in Australia.

My lived experiences

Childhood: Experiences at schools

I was able to access education in schools where English was the medium of instruction. My parents, although self-made without any support from my grandparents, could make ends meet because my father worked for India's central government entities. In those days, this meant that employment and income was ongoing. Although my mother was married at a very young age, by the time I was born, she was in her early 30s and managing a business venture. This made my family economically able to support my education at private schools rather than government (or public) schools.

My school life was not all that great. Almost every other transgender person would have had similar if not the same school experiences. I attended religious schools, which went by Christian values. When I was six years old or younger, I realised that I was 'like a girl'. Right now, I might use the term 'different'; however, at the time, I felt a lot like a girl as I liked a fellow boy student and wanted him as my boyfriend.

This school was co-educational. It did not really make me feel odd as I thought I was a girl although I was not wearing skirts. However, when I went back home after school, I would use a bedsheet and drape it around me like a saree and walk around the home in front of my maternal grandmother who cared for the family when my parents worked. This was indeed a very innocent period in my life.

When I completed Year 2, I had to move to another school, also of Christian faith, but further away from home. This was an all-boys school. My academic performance until Year 10 was stellar – I would always achieve within the top three ranks in my class. However, with some perspective, while other boys recognised my femininity because of my voice, intonations, walk and such other mannerisms, my femininity paved the way for me to be humiliated and even molested. I believed then that when these fellow boy students touched my body, it was because they felt and accepted my femininity. I was never taught the term and the meaning of 'molestation'. Could this be because this was a boys-only school? Was this because only girls needed to know the difference between 'good touching' and 'bad touching'?

I spent nine years at this school (1993–2002). It did not and still does not have a support system for trans and gender diverse students. Because all the school alumni are men, it is extremely difficult for me to share my ideas about true gender equality, and sexual and gender diversity.

I recall an incident that really tarnished my image and caused my grades to go down due to depression. In Year 10, I was in love with a classmate who had a huge network of friends and always presented himself as this supremely masculine person – a 'macho'. While I became one of the teachers' favourites academically (which some of my teachers might now

122

refute in favour of their more 'masculine' ex-students), my classmates almost always came top of the class because they were more street-smart and more favoured by the teachers.

The favouritism towards my fellow classmates and their 'macho' nature gave them the courage and audacity to behave the way they did towards me. I developed a habit of keeping a personal diary, where I wrote about being in love with my 'macho' classmate. A group of boys somehow found my diary in my bag and read all my thoughts to everyone including the teachers. Ever since that incident, I have been heartbroken and traumatised. I was seen as a very sensitive person and at times even some teachers took the liberty to mock my gender identity that I was still forming at the time.

The 'macho' cliques were well-connected with some teachers. Some teachers had sons of relatives studying there. While there were exceptionally professional teachers, there were others who stooped so low as to mock a student's gender identity when they got the chance.

Most teachers were women, which is perhaps why they took advantage and humiliated and invalidated the femininity of people like me. These teachers did not and still do not know how to help LGBTQIA+ young people. They are so ill-trained in this aspect even if their subject-level training can be so perfect. These teachers are the ones who teach future leaders and that is a worrying aspect.

For example, there was a guy who was appointed a School Pupil Leader in Year 12 (final year). Teachers picked him for a leadership position because he was their favourite. One day, when he was in Year 11 and I was in Year 10, he approached me (I was having lunch with a friend) and said (translated from Tamil to English): "Hey four-and-a-half and four-and-a-half … give me some water." It was not until much later that I understood the meaning of 'four-and-a-half and four-and-a-half', which adds up to 'nine', a word that is extremely derogatory and used against the being, existence and gender identity of trans people. I did not realise the meaning of this phrase because my parents had sheltered me.

Young adulthood: Final years of school and university life

In my final year, I attended a private boarding school because my father wanted me to repeat Year 12 to study abroad. My experience at this boarding school was horrendous. Everything from the food to the way fellow students treated me, some of whom were from abroad, was awful.

In one incident, a fellow boy student asked me to sit next to him to get the attention of another girl he was infatuated with. He looked at her and made comments while molesting me at the same time. Three or four other boy students joined in as it was fun for them to humiliate an effeminate person like me so long as they could get girls' attention.

The catch here is, if I reacted, they would ask me whether I really had breasts like women. I had to put up with the molestation as I could only react if I did have breasts. Then everyone would 'out' me as a girl, and that news would reach my parents who would punish me or worse. So, I remained silent.

Another girl student from overseas humiliated me for no reason at all in front of many students. She was younger and she said that she was interested in me. However, I did not respond positively. In refusing her, I was at great risk because of her connections. I was determined to endure all of this alone. If my parents came to know I was transgender, that would be the day when I brought disgrace to my family. My parents would punish me severely and my future educational dreams would never come true.

Another incident tested my endurance. Two boy students found me one night after school and demanded sexual favours. They blackmailed me that they would 'out' me to the teacher and then my parents would know. I was very scared. They took me up to the top floor of the school but decided to return to my room, which had a lock. By the time the sexual activity could take place, there were noises indicating that someone was coming, and I took this opportunity to rush out from that place. Ever since that time, those two boys kept a close eye on me.

I told my parents that this was not a safe place for me. The next day, my father came to the school and tasted the food. He decided then that my boarding would end that very moment. He asked me how and why I put up with such bad conditions. I was just happy to leave and did not give away anything but smiled. As my final exams were getting close, my father took great care of me by renting a house in the locality, arranging for extra tuition, and cooking so that I could focus on my exams.

After I successfully completed Year 12, I left for Australia for undergraduate studies with my father's support. My life in Australia was not exactly a bed of roses. Instead, it had its own difficulties beginning with my choice of degree, which an education agent wrongfully influenced. When I reached Sydney, it was all very new, and I found it hard to settle in academically and otherwise. Gradually, once I changed courses and moved closer to Sydney, I was somewhat able to manage.

However, my personal life, especially my gender identity and sexual orientation, was still at crisis point. I did not know where I belonged. I was so much in need of love and care. I was hoping to find true love. I was naïve of the immigration rules and regulations. I tried my luck on dating apps to meet as many men as possible. I was scared to show my trans-ness, fearing that I might attract the wrong kind of men who could get violent. Hence, I maintained my gender identity as a man and my sexual orientation as gay. I was so confused that despite having access to gay bars and pubs and other such venues in Sydney, I never exactly felt comfortable.

I decided to see a psychologist. On the day of the appointment, I was at Hyde Park. At this juncture, I decided to take a drastic step to change my entire life. I called my parents. I told them I was attracted to men only and felt gay. My father's advice was that since I was in Australia for my studies, I should focus on that while exploring and experimenting with my sexuality whenever I could.

Unfortunately, my mother to this day neither understands nor accepts the fact that I am a non-heterosexual and will never be marrying a ciswoman. This is because, to her, I was and still am her only dear son on whom she had a lot of 'masculine' expectations such as marrying a ciswoman and having a family of my own.

When I met the psychologist, I mentioned what my father had said, and it took the psychologist by surprise because of my Indian background. However, my father was known to have liberal thoughts despite his conservative rural background. For example, he allowed my sister to marry a man whom she fell in love with despite much opposition because he was from another religion and caste. My father understood how a progressive way of life would benefit his children.

I lived in Australia between 2004 and 2007. Although this time was rewarding, it was particularly hard. I was naïve, trying to understand myself and others' expectations, trying to make ends meet while managing academic and professional expectations. I did not really have friends. It was very difficult to get connected into the webs of friendship as a newcomer.

Even now in Melbourne, existing communities are seldom welcoming. When I wanted to get in touch with a queer ethnic community, I found its members to be very cold, unhelpful and unwelcoming. People who have already been here for a few years want to be known as the only members of the group. Very recently, a Canadian-born Gujarati Australian discriminated against me by saying that neither he nor his housemates would allow me to rent a room in his house, which is close to my university, because they do not like transgender people and people of other such 'new' genders. This is despite him being a bisexual cisman and one of his housemates being a gay cisman. Most rental providers are either racist or transphobic or both, making life harder for trans and gender diverse international students like me.

Middle and later adulthood: After my university degree

My experimentation with my sexuality continued throughout university life. I returned to India in 2007 and began a bachelor's degree in psychology. Many students wanted to become friends when they found out that I had lived in Australia. This meant that I was under scrutiny all the time, at least by the student body. I graduated first in my degree despite fierce competition.

I had the support of my parents and was an all-rounder at college. I also participated in extracurricular activities.

Some students seemed to be attracted to my femininity. I did not disclose to my close friends that I belonged to the LGBTQIA+ community. One heterosexual guy was very friendly. There was nothing sexual. I went to his house and met his parents, who loved me. I was looking for a true and trustworthy friend. But he only wanted to make friends because of the good-looking women in the psychology department where I was studying. Unfortunately, to this guy, I was not even human. This broke me.

There was this one guy who proposed to me, despite his religion and family being against such practices. I was so happy that I had finally met the love of my life. But I had doubts about the motives behind this guy's 'love' because he once told me he was blown away by my beauty when I wore tight bell-bottom jeans to college. He said he kept staring at my body parts.

All my life, I longed for love from a male romantic partner. When this guy wanted to marry me, I was elated and trusted him so much. The fact that he might have just fallen for my body did not factor in. I had dreamt of spending the rest of my life with this guy, but he slowly started avoiding me. We were not involved sexually. However, I was so tied to him emotionally. During a phone call, he admitted he was engaged to someone else and wanted to sever ties with me. I was heartbroken that he would do this to me.

I sought help from a renowned psychiatrist. I took a heterosexual friend with me, who did not want to be there. My father was also there. Unfortunately, this psychiatrist did not have any empathy and was not sensitised about LGBTQIA+ communities and lived experiences. The worst part is that this psychiatrist was against sexual and gender diversity. I went to see this psychiatrist as I was extremely depressed and could not overcome that agony. The psychiatrist said he would talk to my father about gay men. At that time, I was only open to my parents about being gay but not as a transgender person let alone a transwoman. The psychiatrist told my father that most of his gay clients got married to women and asked another man – a relative or a stranger – to have sex with their spouses. These discussions hugely disgusted me. I was fearful of how these ideas may shape my father's views of LGBTQIA+ communities. I wanted to be by myself to be myself – someone between an effeminate gay man and a transwoman.

I worked in Chennai, Bengaluru and later in Hyderabad. While I had the freedom to do anything I wanted, it was difficult to manage co-workers, particularly in Hyderabad. The work culture was extremely bad. Some of the employees including my manager used to mock me. My line manager and colleagues humiliated me in front of others. I received all the blame when I complained, so I resigned. I took a break from work. I did not see myself fitting into that sort of shallow environment and decided to pursue an academic career.

I wanted to make a difference in society in my own way as a well-renowned researcher with a PhD. While I studied for a master's in development policy and practice, it was challenging, and I had no friends. But I was grateful that some academic staff were supportive. I published in prestigious journals and became the editor-in-chief for one of India's foremost news journals. I put my research plans on hold because of the COVID-19 pandemic. I then worked for a large Indian government (Ministry of Education) funded project at a university in Tiruchirappalli (Trichy), Tamil Nadu.

My stay in Trichy gave me newfound freedom. As a Project Fellow, I met a lot of good people. Although I had to pass as a cisman to get accommodation just like how I do now in Melbourne, I came out to my supervisor, work colleagues and a couple of housemates. It was particularly difficult to handle people at work as many were insensitive, not just towards sexual and gender diversity but also to the whole concept of gender itself. Because my supervisor was a leader in gender research, I felt safe bringing forth new ideas to impact behavioural changes among my work colleagues. I worked with 30 cismen and ciswomen. I was the only transwoman/transfemme person and Thirunangai.

When the project staff were preparing a baseline survey for the Census 2011, neither they nor the team leader paused to think about including questions on sexual and gender diversity. I pushed for sexual and gender diversity to be included but the issue was not taken very seriously. I had to come out to many team members to make them understand that it was cruel to exclude people like me just because of their ignorance about sexual and gender diversity. I felt it was important for researchers especially to be unbiased towards sexual and gender diversity.

Incidentally, I met a few transwomen who all lived together in Trichy. I made friends and the clan welcomed me as part of their chosen family. It was like having a safe sanctuary to express my femininity, which I was unable to do at my own place. I would hang out with my trans family after work and return to my room to sleep. Fortunately, they lived quite close. I was the oldest member in this trans clan (others were in their early 20s). Apart from one person, all the others were at some stage or level of transitioning, which I was not. This at times gave room for a couple of other transwomen in the clan to discount and invalidate my femininity by saying that I am not trans or trans enough.

Sometimes, they also doubted my commitment to the clan. The word 'commitment' is important here because there are certain rules and norms, or in my understanding, a level of victimisation that I had to agree to be subjected to, to belong to a trans clan. This starts with an adoption ceremony called a 'Reeth' function. Every new transwoman is to be adopted by an elder in the community to receive guidance and support, especially for the 'nirvanam' or the gender reassignment surgery. This surgery costs money, which new transwomen were mostly unable to afford as they might have run away from home and were unemployed or underemployed because of their supposedly lesser qualifications.

The 'Guru-Chela' system plays a vital role in shaping the entire community of transwomen on the Indian subcontinent. The 'Guru' is the adopter and mother, and guide to the 'Chela' who is the adopted daughter and disciple. The Guru is also like a husband or an alpha-man in the relationship. To be part of the system, it is necessary that all transwomen have undergone surgeries. If they are unable to, they take a backseat in the Jamaat, which is the family system where all the transwomen of a chosen family come together, meet and resolve everyday issues.

If a transwoman has not undergone gender reassignment surgery, then their femininity is often discounted and invalidated. As many new transwomen may be unable to fund their gender reassignment surgery, quite often the Guru helps the Chela, who must pledge themselves for *basthi* (begging) or *thanda* (sex work). For many, this is the opportunity they have all been yearning for – the opportunity to become a full woman through gender reassignment surgery. Some people refuse gender reassignment surgery vehemently because of their body conditions or their family situations.

I am one of those who discourages and refuses gender reassignment surgery because of body conditions and family situations. Although I too yearn to affirm my gender identity, I aim to spread body positivity. Because of this approach towards my gender identity, I get excluded from my own community. However, in the trans family in Trichy, I found the Guru very inclusive and understanding rather than imposing gender reassignment surgery, sex work and begging as conditions for me to be part of this family.

I gave the members of this trans family an opportunity to share their lived experiences at a work event that I organised, to encourage behavioural changes among the mainstream community including my colleagues and among 'other' transwomen. At the event, a cisgender heterosexual man who was a postdoctoral research fellow in social work took over and spoke entirely about his lived experience. He did not allow the guest speakers to share their experiences at all and took the entire scheduled time for himself: "I am a *researcher* and I am a social worker and I know more than even they may know" (emphasis added). This shocked me but I had to remain silent because he was a senior researcher.

This incident sparked a great interest in me to become a renowned researcher on transgender and gender diverse issues in India and across the world as a Thirunangai, gender non-binary and trans person. For far too long, lived experiences of non-binary and gender diverse and trans people have been presented from an outsider perspective. Cis-gender folks have taken advantage of gender diverse and trans people not being represented in academia to benefit themselves and their careers.

An incident in early 2022 throughout Tamil Nadu forced me to leave my job. A journalist who transited through Trichy visited the Central Bus

Depot and noticed many used condoms. They published a video on social media (TamilFront, 2021) accusing transwomen solely of doing sex work in Trichy and ruining the Tamil community and culture. This triggered a major argument in my workplace, and no one supported me. A week or so later, the Honorable Supreme Court of India, in one of its landmark rulings, recognised sex work as a profession (Chowdhury, 2022).

Motivation for a research career

My experiences as a transwoman/transfemme have paved the way towards establishing a research career for myself. Despite the care and support that I received from my parents, all I have received from the outside, heteropatriarchal, bio-normative world is hate, humiliation and hurt. This is common among many transgender people across cultures, languages and geographical boundaries. I am not immune to this.

When I saw the awful treatment of transgender and non-binary people, and especially transwomen among my own colleagues, I felt an urgent need to become a researcher. For me, this means that I will be able to deconstruct and demystify translations and interpretations of stories of gender diverse and trans souls from the perspective(s) of cisgender and heterosexual researchers who have not and will never have the lived experiences of gender diverse and trans souls, however noble their intentions may be.

Researchers from western and white-majority countries have published most of the research about trans and gender diverse people, especially from majority-world countries such as India. While these teams may include one or two researchers from India, the latter would rarely lead the projects. Even if they did, they may not be a trans and gender diverse person. This may be because of the lack of representation of such researchers, especially in the Indian context.

Some of the existing research about trans and gender diverse people has only problematised and pathologised their lives (T'Sjoen et al, 2020; Rogers, 2021). Pathologisation refers to intentionally labelling and treating trans and gender diverse people's self-identified gender, body, gender expression or presentation, and the agency or practice of gender identity, as abnormal or deviant (Rogers, 2021). This constant pathologising only increases stigma against, marginalisation and social isolation of trans and gender diverse people. It also invalidates and invisibilises their lived experiences and silences their perspectives (Anzani et al, 2021). Pathologisation is often faced as microaggressions (Mizock and Lundquist, 2016), that is, subtle forms of everyday interactions that affect individuals. Transgender-specific microaggressions take place on different levels (Anzani et al, 2019; 2021), for example, through the assumption of transgender experiences as universal, or trans and gender diverse people being exoticised for researchers' career benefits along with denial and masking of researchers' own transphobia.

The invisibilisation and silencing of voices of Indigenous trans and gender diverse people and their cultures by means of colonial and western-centric interpretations is another major issue. Such interpretations have imposed hierarchies that privilege knowledge from western and white-majority countries as global, while labelling knowledge from countries such as India as Indigenous, contextualising it to a specific time and place (Chatterjee, 2018). Thus, promoting research careers among trans and gender diverse people from a range of countries is of paramount importance.

I am determined to pursue a research career to be among those at the forefront of this change that could possibly encourage more Indigenous trans and gender diverse people especially from majority-world countries such as India. I have come full circle as I recently began my PhD in Australia.

Suggestions for researchers

Much of the research on trans and gender diverse people reflects the perspectives of researchers who are not trans or gender diverse, interpreting lived experiences from their positionalities (Galupo, 2017). While there is a steady rise in the number of transgender researchers publishing on various topics pertinent to the lives and experiences of trans and gender diverse people in western contexts, this is still a distant reality in majority-world countries such as India (Veale, 2017). The representation of trans and gender diverse people in research communities is crucial because researchers who are not trans and gender diverse can fail these communities (Dinno et al, 2013). Hence, researchers who are cisgender must make way for increased representation of trans and gender diverse researchers. Mere interest in the plight of trans and gender diverse people may not be enough for cisgender and heterosexual researchers to pursue research on trans and gender diverse people.

Similar to the views of an openly trans psychology lecturer, Dr Jaimie Veale (University of Waikato, Aotearoa New Zealand), one of the benefits of ceding space for representation of trans and gender diverse researchers in academia is to demystify the notion that trans and gender diverse people are mere participants or subjects or patients in a study or inquiry (Galupo, 2017). Trans and gender diverse researchers positively impact how knowledge is generated as a result of explorations on transgender issues in line with professional standards such as the World Professional Association for Transgender Health. But even at the best conferences about the sexual health of LGBTQIA+ people, trans researchers have shared their experiences of being pathologised through, for example, misgendering, or not providing adequate interpreting and translation support for a transgender therapist who shared their lived experience (Scheim et al, 2019).

I reiterate the suggestions for cisgender researchers who pursue research with trans and gender diverse people (see Scheim et al, 2019) that cisgender researchers have an ethical obligation to recognise and address the power structures in their projects. Research teams should disclose these details when seeking funding to pursue research with trans and gender diverse people. Cisgender researchers should pay attention to the gender composition of teams to include trans and gender diverse researchers when transgender communities are involved. Where there is inequitable representation of trans and gender diverse researchers, cisgender researchers should decline invitations to publish or present at conferences. Cisgender researchers should instead promote trans and gender diverse researchers as project leaders and support their travel. Funding should be allocated for professional translation to enable trans and gender diverse researchers to use the language they are most comfortable in.

Notes

[1] Trans people are often scrutinised and assessed if they are trans enough to even exercise their fundamental human rights. The focus on change rather than realisation makes transitioning through surgery a societal expectation that needs to be met.

[2] Throughout this chapter, I consciously use the words transwoman/transwomen and transfemme instead of trans woman/trans women and trans femme. I use the former denotations of my gender identity to consciously disrupt the usual academic forms which I believe is an imposition of trans exclusionary agenda founded on western thoughts.

Further reading

Bala, P. (2019) 'The marginalized neither male nor female with reference to truth about me: A hijra life story by Revathi', *Rock Pebbles: Indian Journal of Language and Literary Criticism*, 28(4): 47–55.

Chakrapani, V., Newman, P.A., Shunmugam, M., McLuckie, A. and Melwin, F. (2007) 'Structural violence against kothi-identified men who have sex with men in Chennai, India: A qualitative investigation', *AIDS Education and Prevention*, 19(4): 346–364.

De Oliveira Ramos, R.C. (2018) 'The voice of an Indian transwoman: A hijra autobiography', *Indi@logs*, 5: 71–88.

Mani, A. (2019) *Overview of Quality of Life of Older Lesbians and Transwomen in India*. Available from: https://osf.io/dya4u [Accessed 17 October 2023].

Mount, L. (2017) '"I am not a hijra": Transwomen claiming citizenship in South India', PhD thesis, Syracuse, Syracuse University.

References

Anzani, A., Morris, E.R. and Galupo, M.P. (2019) 'From absence of microaggressions to seeing authentic gender: Transgender clients' experiences with microaffirmations in therapy', *Journal of LGBT Issues in Counselling*, 13(4): 258–275.

Anzani, A., Sacchi, S. and Pruna, A. (2021) 'Microaggressions towards lesbian and transgender women: Biased information gathering when working alongside gender and sexual minorities', *Journal of Clinical Psychology*, 77(9): 2027–2040.

Bourke, B. (2014) 'Positionality: Reflecting on the research process', *The Qualitative Report*, 19(33): 1–9.

Chatterjee, S. (2018) 'Transgender shifts: Notes on resignification of gender and sexuality in India', *TSQ: Transgender Studies Quarterly*, 5(3): 311–320.

Chowdhury, K. (2022) 'India's supreme court recognizes sex work as a profession', *The Diplomat*. Available from: https://thediplomat.com/2022/06/indias-supreme-court-recognizes-sex-work-as-a-profession/ [Accessed 22 November 2022].

Dinno, A., Franks, M.C., Burleton, J. and Smith, T.C. (2013) 'On the just and accurate representation of transgender persons in research', *Community Health Faculty Publications and Presentations*, 39: 1–18.

Galupo, M.P. (2017) 'Researching while cisgender: Identity considerations for transgender research', *International Journal of Transgenderism*, 18(3): 241–242.

Holman Jones, S., Adams, T.E and Ellis, C. (eds) (2015) *Handbook of Autoethnography*, Oxon and New York: Routledge.

Hopkins, R.M., Regehr, G. and Pratt, D.D. (2016) 'A framework for negotiating positionality in phenomenological research', *Medical Teacher*, 39(1): 20–25.

Koopman W.J., Watling C.J. and LaDonna K.A. (2020) 'Autoethnography as a strategy for engaging in reflexivity', *Global Qualitative Nursing Research*, 19(7): 2333393620970508.

Mizock, L. and Lundquist, C. (2016) 'Missteps in psychotherapy with transgender clients: Promoting gender sensitivity in counseling and psychological practice', *Psychology of Sexual Orientation and Gender Diversity*, 3(2): 148–155.

Rogers, M.M. (2021) 'Exploring the domestic abuse narratives of trans and nonbinary people and the role of cisgenderism in identity abuse, misgendering, and pathologizing', *Violence Against Women*, 27(12–13): 2187–2207.

Scheim, A.I., Appenroth, M.N., Beckham, S.W., Goldstein, Z., Grinspan, M.C., Keatley, J.G. and Radix, A. (2019) 'Transgender HIV research: Nothing about us without us', *The Lancet*, 6(9): e566–567.

Secules, S., McCall, C., Mejia, J.A., Beebe, C., Masters, A.S., Sánchez-Peña, M.L. and Svyantek, M. (2021) 'Positionality practices and dimensions of impact on equity research: A collaborative inquiry and call to the community', *Journal of Engineering Education*, 110(1): 19–43.

TamilFront (2021) திருச்சியில் அமோகமாக நடைபெறும் விபச்சாரம்! | மூட்டை மூட்டையாக Condom! | இரவு நேர ஜல்சா! TamilFront.

Transgender Persons (Protection of Rights) Act (2019) No. 40, India: Indiacode. Available from: https://www.indiacode.nic.in/bitstream/123456789/13091/1/a2019-40.pdf [Accessed 25 June 2023].

T'Sjoen, G., Radix, A. and Motmans, J. (2020) 'Language & ethics in transgender health', *Journal of Sexual Medicine*, 17(9): 1585–1586.

Veale, J.F. (2017) 'Reflections on transgender representation in academic publishing', *International Journal of Transgenderism*, 18(2): 121–122.

Wiesner, A. (2018) 'Autoethnography: Beyond the gender binary through writing lives', *Glasnik Etnografskog instituta*, 66(2): 335–346.

Williams, N. (2021) *Autoethnography: A Decolonizing Research Methodological Approach*, Thousand Oaks: SAGE.

Zaharin, A. and Pallotta-Chiarolli, M. (2022) 'Reclaiming transgender identity through intersectionality and decoloniality: A critical autoethnography of an academic-activist performance', *Journal of Intercultural Studies*, 43(1): 98–119.

8

Responding collaboratively to COVID-19 and our health needs across Pacific communities: CORE Pacific Collective

Jioji Ravulo, Seini Afeaki, Malaemie Fruean, Donina Va'a and Maherau Arona

Key points

- This chapter disrupts the academy by highlighting the value of *talanoa* as a culturally centred and community-led research and knowledge creation process.
- Privileging Pasifika perspectives provides a platform for effective and engaging health and community responses developed with local Pacific-Indigenous peoples alongside their support services and social structures.
- Lived experience knowledge that informs applied research activities helps understand the situations and circumstances Pacific people may be situated and located within.
- By co-creating, co-curating and co-opting this knowledge, it can help mobilise a leadership approach alongside social inclusion outcomes that are grounded in a collective, collegial and collaborative approach.
- Social justice tenets around access, equity, participation and human rights can be enacted through a culturally nuanced and relevant approach.

Introduction

This chapter is co-authored by five Pasifika peoples, also known as Pacific-Indigenous and First Nations Pacific. We reflect on our own lived experiences and journey as professionals striving to work in partnership across the local region and beyond. We endeavour to decolonise and disrupt how we co-create knowledge that can inform applied research activities and lead to social justice outcomes for diverse communities. We have employed a collective, collaborative and collegial approach through a *talanoa* process, where we share and hold a dialogically driven space to talk about our experience of working together to support our Pasifika communities through the CORE (Collaboration Openness Respect Empowerment) Pacific Collective.

Talanoa is a key concept found across Pacific-Indigenous cultures, which allows for a collective and shared conversation with no prescribed agenda or structure (Vaioleti, 2013). Rather, it aims to create a safe space for participants to hold space, to sit within space, and to share their own insights on topics explored (Farrelly and Nabobo-Baba, 2014). As a relational approach, a *talanoa* provides people with an opportunity to nurture the sacred (*vā* or *tabu*) connection they have with self and others (Tecun et al, 2018). Authenticity is a major component in creating a *talanoa* that is sincere. Participants are actively invited to be vulnerable on the premise that others will. As a result, a deep sense of connection is established, providing the platform to establish and share themes organically. We write this chapter as a shared conversation with ourselves and readers, as an approach of working together by sharing knowledge.

First formed in June 2021, the CORE Pacific Collective came together to collaboratively respond to COVID-19-related concerns raised by Pacific people across Greater Western Sydney in the state of New South Wales (NSW). We represent the top five Pacific diasporas in Australia: Māori, Cook Islander, Samoan, Tongan and Fijian. Three main issues were raised: first, Pasifika communities had limited information and understandings of the impacts of COVID-19; second, there was a need to promote the safety and effectiveness of getting vaccinated; and third, we aimed to reinforce that their spiritual, religious and traditional cultural practices can complement westernised medical treatments. As a group, we mobilised key activities alongside key collaborators, including NSW Health, NSW Multiculturalism and local community-based agencies. We developed a series of videos in Pacific-Indigenous languages to share across our social media platforms; we helped host vaccination hubs in community centres in suburbs across Greater Western Sydney; we provided media commentary and opinion pieces; we hosted weekly Facebook Live events titled 'Nurturing Vā' with experts and government representatives to interact with our communities; and we developed a HOPE COVID-19 toolkit that provides practical resources in language for our communities. Our work is housed under a dedicated website.[1]

It is through this shared approach that our lived experience led to the co-creation, co-curation and co-opting of knowledge and research that shaped and continues to inextricably influence our activities, outputs and outcomes. All of our resources were developed alongside experts in various academic fields, including medicine, social work, nursing, public health, educational leadership and exercise sciences, so that they would also learn to work collaboratively with our community groups to achieve social justice.

We first reflect on literature that discusses the importance of shaping lived experience-led knowledge towards social justice outcomes. This is followed by our *talanoa* that we held in person and audio-recorded in Fairfield, NSW, Australia, in May 2022. This *talanoa* was an opportunity for us to reflect on our work to consolidate and catapult future direction as a collective entity.

At the same time, we are keen to express how our lived experiences as Pasifika people shaped our shared approach to responding to community needs. This knowledge was curated as a means to mobilise current and future social action and change.

Writing this chapter as a form of collaborative autoethnography

We use collaborative autoethnography to formally document and reflect on the shared work of the CORE Pacific Collective. In accordance with Chang and colleagues (2016), collaborative autoethnography is an opportunity to create shared understanding of experiences that may occur with groups working together. This solicits a broader perspective on the phenomena being examined, while also positioning such lived experience as tangible research evidence and outcomes. The iterative process of a collaborative autoethnography involves four steps (Chang et al, 2016):

1. Preliminary data collection: group sharing and probing.
2. Subsequent data collection: group sharing and preliminary meaning-making.
3. Data analysis and interpretation: group meaning-making and theme search.
4. Report writing: group writing.

In essence, we engaged in collaborative autoethnography where our *talanoa* (shared conversation) was used for step 1, preliminary data collection. In writing up the transcript of the *talanoa*, we undertook step 2, subsequent data collection, where we further explored the context and shape of our shared conversation and assigned preliminary meaning to what we discussed. We moved to step 3, data analysis and interpretation through the key themes derived directly from the transcript of the talanoa, which led to the subsequent and final step 4, the group writing of this chapter.

We were able to achieve the anticipated benefits of collaborative autoethnography (Chang et al, 2016), including the collective explorations of researcher subjectivity, power sharing among researcher-participants, efficiency and enrichment in the research process, deeper learning about self and others, and supporting community building. As such, we see the potential for culturally centred and community-led research to generate tangible outcomes including influencing policy and practice and for further knowledge creation.

Reflections from the literature

The literature we accessed to support our understanding of lived experience-led knowledge and research was mostly grounded in health settings and social services. Mental health treatment and recovery practices have benefited from the role of peer workers, who are employed based on their own lived experience of mental distress. These knowledges help shape and ground nuanced recovery strategies (Honey et al, 2020). This has disrupted the status quo of the medical model, which is privileged as the underlying premise to health systems and structures. Effective leadership can assist in promoting lived experience in practice settings to create a sustained and meaningful approach (Byrne et al, 2018).

As a methodology, lived experience-led research provides a platform for individual voices to be part of a broader conversation, nuanced with insights on how people experience their own space and place (Petitmengin et al, 2019). It helps make meaning of the micro (individual and families), meso (community and organisational) and macro (systems and structures) challenges and disrupts dominant discourses that perpetuate and take for granted the realities of people who are not in positions of influence and power (Frechette et al, 2020). There is a push for academic institutions to better support researchers with lived experience so that their knowledge is valued, through professional pipelines and academic roles (Jones et al, 2021).

From a social policy perspective, the lived experience approach has been undervalued, and might not appeal to people outside the social sciences (McIntosh and Wright, 2019). However, other disciplines including the medical sciences are starting to use lived experience perspectives to shape responses that go beyond the goal of a one-size-fits-all health approach. This suggests that there are multiple, and even more complex ways, to creating solutions. Social and health services that interact with people based on their development stage, such as childhood, can be greatly assisted in their effectiveness and engagement when children are given an opportunity to shape their care outcomes through lived experience (Rogoff et al, 2018).

From a Pacific point of view, exploring and examining our lived experiences as a Pasifika diaspora in Australia is vital. Our prevalence and presence have been maligned by over-representation in youth justice spaces (Ravulo, 2016a; 2016b) and under-representation in higher education (Ravulo, 2019). Our mental health needs and accompanying levels of health literacy has impacted our engagement with health services and help-seeking behaviours (Ravulo et al, 2021). Failure to understand our realities will continue to perpetuate lack of inclusion across health settings, leading to poorer social and economic outcomes.

The context of COVID-19 emphasised the need for researchers to use qualitative methodologies to shape medical treatments (Gorna et al, 2021). Without understanding the lived experience of Pasifika people at the onset of COVID-19, Australian responses failed to recognise the need to create knowledge and research to assist in counteracting misinformation and hesitancy in treatment. A lack of insight into the shared reality of minority groups, especially those based on class, ethnicity and colour, or even combined and intersecting all three, leads to poorer health outcomes and large disparities in accessing treatment (Lopez et al, 2021).

Our *talanoa* as the CORE Pacific Collective

Malo e lelei, Seini Finau Afeaki is my name, from the Kingdom of Tonga. Finau is my maiden name. I was born and raised in the village of Masilamea, on the main island of Tongatapu. My maternal grandparents are from Pangai Ha'apai, Nukunuku and Kolomotu'a and my paternal grandparents are from Masilamea. I am a fearless advocate with a purpose for the Pacific communities in NSW for the last 30-plus years. I started my career in Tonga as a teacher at Queen Salote College, my old high school. I later joined the Ministry of Finance as the Deputy Secretary and migrated to Australia in 1984. Since then, I have worked across government and non-government agencies in different capacities, and I am currently with the NSW Children's Court Clinic. My postgraduate training is on project management and policy development. I have served on different boards including as a former Commissioner for the NSW Community Relations Commission. I am currently a Senior Advisor to the Pacific Women's Professional Business Network. I am also the Chairperson of the Pacific Mental Health Initiative.

Pacific greetings and *talofa lava*, I am Loau Donina Va'a, Early Childhood Development Specialist Consultant with UNICEF Pacific, providing technical support to the Pacific Regional Council for Early Childhood Development, and Chair of the Pacific Women's Professional Business Network. My father hails from Saoluafata, Upolu, and my mother from Sala'ilua, Savai'i. Born in Grey Lynn, New Zealand, I grew up in Samoa and Fiji. Most of my professional life is in Sydney, though I have also worked in Samoa, Fiji and New Zealand.

Kia orana! Warm Pacific greetings, I am Maherau Arona. I was born in Dunedin, New Zealand. My father is from Rakahanga, and my mother is from Penryhn, Cook Islands. I am married to Toa Arona from Tupapa Village. My Piho family home is Matavera. I currently reside in Sydney. I am employed with a non-government agency called Mission Australia and I also work as a Youth Justice Conference Convenor. I am the President of the Pacific Islands Mount Druitt Action Network Incorporated and Team Manager for the Cook Islands Rugby League Women's World Cup Team that competed in the UK in November 2022. I studied at Otago University, and worked for New Zealand's Department of Child, Youth and Family Services.

Kia Ora. Ko Malaemie Fruean toku ingoa (Greetings. My name is Malaemie Fruean). I am the Chair of the NSW Council for Pacific Communities. Both my mother and father are from Ngapuhi associated with the Northland region of Aotearoa New Zealand and centred in the Hokianga, the Bay of

Islands, and Whangārei. I was born and raised in Whangarei, New Zealand – my *whānau* (family) is from Whangaruru Ngatiwai; we are the children of the sea. I have lived in Australia now for over 37 years, most of that time in Sydney where I still currently reside with my husband Charlie, our five children and 12 grandchildren. Charlie is New Zealand born Samoan; his mother is from the village of Mulifanua and his father from the village of Faatoia. I have worked within the community for a number of years doing community development. I have been employed by TAFE NSW (technical college), Mission Australia, Campbelltown City Council, One Door Mental Health and now I manage the South West Multicultural and Community Centre. I have a BA in adult education from the University of Technology Sydney. In 2021, I was awarded the Order of Australia Medal. I am very humbled and honoured to have received this recognition for the service I have been blessed to do with Pacific communities in NSW. The following Māori proverb reflects my approach: *He aha te mea nui o te ao* (What is the most important thing in the world?) *He tangata, he tangata, he tangata* (It is the people, it is the people, it is the people).

Bula and G'day, I'm Jioji Ravulo, Professor and Chair of Social Work and Policy Studies at the University of Sydney. My father is iTaukei (Indigenous) Fijian, with his father coming from Nayavuira village in the region of Ra, and mother from Sawani in the region of Naitasiri. My late mother is Anglo-Australian and originally from Sydney. I was born and raised in Sydney, Australia, and have lived and worked most of my personal and professional life in various areas of Greater Western Sydney. My academic life has included working with the University of the South Pacific, providing opportunities to collaborate across the Pacific.

Collectively, we would like to acknowledge the traditional owners of the land, the Cabrogal people of the Darug nation, in which this *talanoa* took place in South West Sydney. We acknowledge that the lands where we work, play and live are all still considered stolen, as sovereignty was never ceded. Always was, always will be Aboriginal land. As Pacific-Indigenous peoples, we strive to be allies and to ensure Aboriginal and Torres Strait Islander peoples and their knowledges, perspectives and practices are privileged across the shared spaces and places we traverse.

In this *talanoa*, we discuss seven key questions that were developed to help us collectively and organically discuss our cultural views and values on our communitys' lived experiences of COVID-19, while subsequently reflecting on the work we have done on this journey together so far.

Why do we do what we do?

Seini: In a nutshell, when they listen, I'll stop what I'm doing. This includes advocacy, lobbying for my community.

So when they sit up and listen, then I will stop. At the moment, they are not listening, so it's not going to stop yet. It's a long journey and process.

Donina: To make change, progress, you need to be seen to exist, and that's absolutely critical to be heard, 'cause then you do exist.

Maherau: I love my community, I love our Pasifika people, and I know in Australia we are over-represented in various areas including youth justice, corrective services. There are lots of issues for our Pasifika community, and I can see there is no beauty in any of that, but we are beautiful people. When this changes and can be seen by the wider Australian community, then we won't stop until we see that. We have a long way to go, but we will do that.

Malaemie: To make a difference, including hope. I acknowledge the mentors that I have had the privilege to walk alongside, including Aunty Molly, who would say 'you are digging the trenches and it's hard work'. I am doing this for my children, your children, for our grandchildren.

Jioji: I do this because I'm passionate about inclusion and passionate about people who are not given the opportunity to have a voice, to have a voice and to be involved in having shared conversations. I'm greatly inspired and encouraged by others along the way that also helps me to keep focused and grounded on what I do and why I do what I do.

What has COVID-19 meant for us?

Seini: Generally, on a personal level, it meant pause, slow down. Self-care was quite prominent at that time, not just for myself, but for my family, my friends, and others and the community. It was a time to pause, reflect and do what you could do for yourself, your family, friends, community. On a community level, I saw what it was doing to our community. It was a time of panic. We as a group put our hands up to do something about it, in response to that panic and requests from individuals being raised to us. It was an opportunity to put our resources together and put aside our indifferences on previous experiences. There were challenges, and some community members weren't understanding what the collective was doing – but we still worked together with the whole community, in guidance from our Elders and in collaboration with the government.

Maherau: I remember the time when the first [Pasifika] mother passed away, and the whole matter went viral via mainstream media and across social media platforms. Because nobody really knew what was going to happen amongst our community. It became very real, very quickly, to hear and see someone so young, with children, die from COVID-19. But our team was able to then access the resources and the support. From the connection that we were able to hook into, including Joseph [La Posta, Chief Executive Officer] from Multicultural NSW, I ended up talking with Western Sydney Local Health District Chief Executive Officer to get a response from public health. It made us work harder, and smarter, as a collective, and because we have power in our own entities, so when we come together as CORE, it made us stronger and made government see their role in supporting and helping to then respond to our families. This approach has then spread locally to the community. As a result, I now have a wonderful relationship with Mt Druitt Police, so much so that I'm talking to the commander of the local office, and it's been built from COVID-19, 'cause they've seen us do this work as a team, as CORE.

Donina: There was a big pause for me too, a renewing of mind and intention on a personal level. Prior to COVID-19, we were running with the wind and then we had to step back to have that pause and look internally as to what's important and what we have to prioritise. What COVID-19 means to me is the relationships, and the sincerity that has evolved from this. The collective is an example of this – where we were able to reach out to organisations including the Muslim Women's Association, Mission Australia and others to support the work that we do 'cause we can't do it ourselves. Despite having our own jobs and families, we were able to pause, come together, put our differences aside and work together. With the fears being felt by the community, we were able to turn it into hope through strategies that the collective were able to implement.

Malaemie: It was like a tsunami for me – as everything was coming our way so quickly. I was feeling overwhelmed, and that's overwhelmed with the requests, and the demands from the community. This was all without looking at your own personal and family stuff. Also, what COVID-19 means for me personally is this unique friendship amongst each other. Whatever pools of resources or networks we had we went to each other's aid to support. And I was a recipient of that too from this group. COVID-19 made me focus on what's really important, which is my family of course, but you're still overwhelmed by the community. Without the CORE Pacific Collective, I don't think I would've coped. Personally, it turned the tide around. My dad has always taught us, when you get caught in the current, don't fight against it, you're going to make yourself tired and you're going to be in danger. You have to go with that current, and without the connection of members, I don't think I would've coped with the current I was in at that time.

Seini: I'm thinking further about how we are all using the word 'connection', 'relationship', 'togetherness' – that's all from our roots, from where we come from. It's who we are. And we are just practising who we are. When it needs to be utilised – we take these approaches out and use them. We are connected people, we are grounded people. We put our heads together and amazingly do and achieve the work.

Jioji: A lot of the stuff around COVID-19 would be about how it separated people, in which it did separate people physically, but on reflection with each other, if I didn't have my involvement with the CORE Pacific Collective, I don't think I would've also come through it because I was also learning so much by virtue of being involved in our activities. I had to turn up, I had to engage, I had to learn about what was happening across the community with COVID-19. Because we were running Nurturing Vā [Facebook Live panel event] where I was facilitating the conversations each week, I had to present, I couldn't take a back seat in this. COVID-19 for me has also meant we were mobilising these relationships, we were also forming a stronger bond with each other, but also helped me to survive COVID-19 personally and with our community.

Why does our lived experience as Pasifika people matter to health outcomes?

Mal: Number one – does it matter? Number two – damn right it matters! We are talking about Pasifika here – so it does matter. We talk about the importance of advocacy and our own voice and the value that the lived experience brings to the table when looking at solutions – which gets you 20 times quicker up the ladder than sitting around going 'well I think, and I think, and I think'. The lived experience should be acknowledged as a strength, not a deficit. That's where the solutions lie.

Donina: No one knows better than the Pacific person themselves, so being able to share that lived experience is important. They know best what they've just gone through – and that will certainly create the awareness from there rather than from somebody else – we need this!

Seini: The lived experience humanises the issue. We just spoke about the first Pacific mother who passed away in Western Sydney – yeah, everybody dies, everywhere. But when you talk about that particular mum and that particular family with those kids, the faces and the stories humanise the issue of COVID-19. The devastation it caused to a person, to kids, to families, to a community – the whole community was devastated by that passing away. Yes, it's about the dollar, it's about the number, but lived experience makes it more meaningful to you, to me and to the policy makers hopefully. So, it makes a difference because your own narrative determines your health outcomes.

Maherau: During this whole experience of COVID-19 for me, I have my nephew who almost died from COVID-19 at Westmead Hospital. The experience that I had with him as his main family here in Sydney – to be involved in the health system's response – was amazing. NSW Health were a great support. We were communicating with family, via Zoom, in New Zealand, and also all around Australia and in the Islands. He was in a coma for three months, and he's only just starting back at work this week, only for light duties. He's had a lived experience with COVID-19 and got through it – it is the human side of how we care for each other that needs to be told and shared. The health staff were absolutely blown away because my family were singing to him whilst he was unconscious, over Zoom. He could hear everything – and even his five-year-old daughter and her mother had to come into the special COVID-19 ward as they contracted COVID-19 too. While they were there, there was this little bird that kept coming onto their balcony. And the daughter believed it to be Daddy visiting her – because they couldn't see each other. So, the lived experience that we have as Pasifika people, you can't connect that with Australian white ways here. I know you all get it, I know Indigenous people would be the same, but [white] people won't get it.

Jioji: It's the context in which people exist, it's the human element. It's all about making sense of what it means to be here, and I think for me, lived experience matters from a Pasifika background, or perspective, or the way in which we view the world, because we can't then create strategies, solutions or engagement without those perspectives.

How does Pasifika leadership influence outcomes?

Seini: We need to define the term leader. Personally, that particular term – when it is referred to me, I would outright say that I'm not. I don't think of myself as a Pacific leader although I've been told 'you are!'. I'm still a learner, and I've got Pacific mentors, everyday, and I quote people who I learn from. So for me – I don't know – I would rather the others are labelled a leader but not me. I would like for other people to be the leaders, and I am just the advocate hoping for changes.

Malaemie: They cannot be what they cannot see. I'm talking about COVID-19; we may not identify with the leader title, but we come into this work, and come into this space – and go back to that why. I look at my grandchildren, and think, well one day, we are now all doing the work towards that. But they cannot be what they cannot see. So, we had to get into the current and step forward regardless of what title we had or did not have. For the community, they needed to see people step forward. I don't think any of us said 'we will step forward' per se, but rather we went into the current with a view to do our best that we can with the resources that we have to help each other. So how does Pasifika leadership influence outcomes? Well, definitely in the *papalagi* (white) world it makes a difference, it does have a huge influence towards the outcomes. It's all about servant leadership. When you go back to your people, they are happy that you do what you do, but if you can't pick up a tea towel and help out in the kitchen – that's what matters to your *whānau* (family). That you haven't forgotten what it's like to serve the people – that's the leadership they are looking for.

Donina:

I see myself as a servant – not as a leader. I'm serving – that's what I love to do. I've always seen leadership as a reflection of my mentors, those that have been there, done that and have paved the way. And that also goes to our Ancestors – I looked to that. That's what's opened doors – I wouldn't be where I am today and I'm hoping to also open doors, and gently pull our people through. So, in regards to influencing change – yes it does – but not per se me – I'm just opening doors that others before me have opened, and I love that. Doors are starting to open, and people are being inclusive of us. Through the collective, I am seeing things that I've never seen before including better changes towards cultural appropriateness. Government departments are taking notice and are wanting to engage productively with us.

Maherau:

We have a lot of leaders in our Pacific communities; we have National Rugby League players who are seen as leaders for the young, we've got ones in music that are seen as leaders in the music world. I'll go into events and young people won't know how I'm connected but their role models do and I'm all good with that. I've always been told off by my husband as I'm the girl when we're in sport, that I would always prefer to run the water bottles onto the field – 'cause I just love serving. I'm one to just do the work and don't see myself as a leader. I know there are times that I have to be a voice for the people, for our community, especially with vaccinations access to our people. Leadership is for the community, for my family. If my children and family succeed, then I've done my duty.

Jioji:

I relate to everything that you are all saying – and that's why we get on so well. Despite how busy we all were, and still are, at no time did I ever take on a request from yourselves and think – no – I can't do it. I did it with a sense of ease and without a sense of burden. I think it's a testament to our shared approach with servant leadership. I too don't see myself as a leader or representative. But by virtue of me turning up in space, from a Pasifika background, that is a point of difference amongst settings that don't have us there. We are disrupting the status quo by turning up.

In Pasifika leadership, we all play a role, we all play a part. In our shared cultural concepts, we all matter, nobody is left behind.

How does the role of gender play out across the community?

Seini: Well, if you look around the CORE Pacific Collective, how many girls are here? Generally during COVID-19, women took the lead in organising and rallying people, whether they are in health, community organisations or on the ground. Women took the lead during COVID-19 in rallying the Pacific community. What did men do – they did a lot too. We called upon our Church leaders, most of them are men, so there are different roles that were interacting during that time. Religious leaders were really good at mobilising their communities for COVID-19 including the community vaccination hubs. Different roles came together. It showed that whatever your gender expression or sexual orientation, we need to do this together. Not one gender can do it.

Malaemie: So, we are the mothers, the nurturers; fathers were the providers. COVID-19 saw gender roles combine to unite and work cohesively with our families during lockdown. The women took a leading role organising things. Whether it was something they were appointed to – it's just their nurturing nature of women. There was a need, and we may not know straight away how to meet the need but actioned straight away something.

Jioji: Gender roles can be quite performative, generally in society, but you see them play out differently in Pacific cultures. Some Pacific cultures are more matriarchal, where women are leaders based on their nurturing and caring roles – and bring this dynamic to a broader community setting and context. I think Pacific men rely heavily on Pacific women to bring that to the conversation and to provide that. We strive to respect and revere women in our lives to work alongside them with a view that everyone plays a part – at the same time it is complementary. By virtue of all genders working together, it reflects the collectivist context in which we operate and exist. Compared to the western perspectives, being able to complement each other through our gender roles is a strength.

Donina: On reflection, we saw women as mothers and nurturers rise to the occasion in getting their families vaccinated. They wanted to also help other families and they started interviewing their children and putting it up on Facebook so that other families could see that it was okay to get vaccinated. The great thing is that you could see the Dad there, in the background, wasn't interviewed, but they went as families. You saw women getting vaccinated, the protectors, and the men would then come. Men walking beside women and their families; it's a win-win situation.

As a result of our collaboration, how have we actioned change?

Donina: Well, we've talked it, we've walked it, we've influenced it. We've certainly walked the talk, and the change. I can't say enough how many people are talking about it – but seeing five people from different Pacific backgrounds, I get asked 'how do you do it?'. There is this mutual respect here, and it was a lack of any hidden agendas. We are here sincerely, for this. Yes – we have our own organisations that we represent – but we all came together to respond; especially when we would use a group call on messenger – we would pick up and talk. Our resources that we developed in collaboration with others is being used across the community including schools and church groups.

Seini: The collective has produced a model that shines a light on who we are as Pacific people. But the collaboration, in itself, we've never really seen in NSW. This is a ground-up thing, by the Pacific people, not a partnership that was instigated by government. It's a framework to be followed by others, cause we've seen it work. We've influenced the change through this model. For the government, they sit up and listen based on collaboration. We got together and governments saw this as an opportunity to engage.

Jioji: I think the change process has been by virtue of us working together collaboratively as five separate entities together to enact and achieve such outcomes.

How does our work reflect and influence social justice?

Seini: If you consider the tenets of social justice, it's about equity, access, participation, diversity and human rights. The CORE Pacific Collective covered all these tenets.

Community was accessing information, diversity is through our representation, having a voice as a basic human right was in supporting our people to participate. Mobilising of resources gave people a chance to get involved and benefit from these shared resources.

Maherau: Where else are you going to see five separate nations, as represented in this group of people, working together voluntarily to enact this change? We are not getting paid to do this work for our communities, for our nations, but I just think there's the richness which in itself says a lot about us being in this space and place together. I don't think you will see this anywhere else in Australia, or New Zealand, especially with what's happening in our communities with all the violence that's happening in the area code. There are five nations in this room working collectively, collaboratively. If the kids in our community could see this – it would be of benefit to all.

Malaemie: Collectively, we have had an influence by all coming together because there was a need. You can't be what you can't see. We think about the young, inspiring leaders that include young women running community-based sessions. It's happening because we have models like the collective that are providing examples and opportunities for others to implement their shared approaches. It's about opening the door for all the others coming through. How many times is it around 'this is mine – I'll get a bit of this and that'. With the collective – it's not about that. It's coming together and not having territorial perspectives or stuff. It's about playing a part in putting together solutions towards turmoil that we are all a part of. Our influence has been in responding practically to the needs of COVID-19, whilst also modelling for young people possibilities to achieve community outcomes to influence social justice. This isn't an elite group – we are in this together.

Donina: We have had our own personal challenges across the pandemic – but as a group we have rallied together to assist each other. The key here is: this hasn't been work, but a passion to support our people. We understood what the issues were by speaking directly to the community. This includes messages we separately received on the issues and concerns, including the fear being felt. It was striving to reflect the voice of the

	community. Our key activities came from trying to alleviate the fears that were being shared with us. As a result, we were able to create support that aimed to meet the need of the community.
Jioji:	I was heartened throughout our journey, seeing this as a support to each other and the wider community. I knew that my contribution would have a contribution to your contribution around this reciprocal context and learning that supported our outputs towards social justice and inclusion. Where everyone was involved, we utilised our strengths to mobilise our shared approach.

Final thoughts from our *talanoa*

From our *talanoa*, we highlighted how our community and culture was at the forefront of our shared responses and work with health services. Without this, we continue to create a limited understanding of the true impacts of health and social issues exacerbated by COVID-19. By working collaboratively, collegially and collectively within Pacific communities, we can mobilise a strength-based approach to shape burgeoning social policy and health service provision. Our lived experiences are at the heart of our narratives and have been the platform to form and facilitate our convictions to be part of the change process towards social justice outcomes.

Our work within a collectivist context is informed by the shared desire to privilege a culturally centred and community-led applied research approach. By centring culturally nuanced perspectives, including those coming directly from lived experience as fellow Pasifika people, we are intentional about this approach. In a western and white framing, failure to work with Pasifika knowledges perpetuates the dysfunction and lack of suitable solutions within health structures, and resources to address Pasifika health needs are mismatched and misaligned. Through our community-led action and activism, we were able to achieve, in real time, health outputs and outcomes that were meaningfully engaging and engaged.

Though reluctant to be seen as leaders or experts, we see the importance of working together as part of our cultural convictions that the collective helps achieve a common good for all. Our diverse lived experiences and different Pasifika heritages have been the platform to shape our contributions to this collaborative approach. We believe that it is through our lived experience that we can help co-create new knowledge across social justice research that deconstructs, disrupts and decolonises dominant academic discourses and its practices. As Pacific-Indigenous people, we are mindful of ensuring our own voices, and as such, representation, should be part of whole-of-community and whole-of-government approaches. Our culturally nuanced views, values, perspectives and practices create spaces that are responsive and engaging, leading to helpful health and welfare outcomes.

Note

[1] See https://www.nswcpc.org.au/core-pacific-collective

Further reading

Cammock, R., Conn, C. and Nayar, S. (2021) 'Strengthening Pacific voices through Talanoa participatory action research', *AlterNative: An International Journal of Indigenous Peoples*, 17(1): 120–129.

Matapo, J. and Enari, D. (2021) 'Re-imagining the dialogic spaces of talanoa through Samoan onto-epistemology', *Waikato Journal of Education*, 26: 79–88.

Ravulo, J., Said, S., Winterstein, U. and New South Wales Ministry of Health (2021) *Mental Health Talanoa (MHT) Research and Resources: Collaborative Community Engagement Enhancing Mental Health and Wellbeing across Pacific Communities*, University of Wollongong. Available from: http://nla.gov.au/nla.obj-2949412205 [Accessed 12 May 2023].

Tunufa'I, L. (2016) 'Pacific research: Rethinking the Talanoa "methodology"', *New Zealand Sociology*, 31(7): 227–239.

References

Byrne, L., Stratford, A. and Davidson, L. (2018) 'The global need for lived experience leadership', *Psychiatric Rehabilitation Journal*, 41(1): 76–79.

Chang, H., Ngunjiri, F. and Hernandez, K.A.C. (2016) *Collaborative Autoethnography*, Oxfordshire: Routledge.

Farrelly, T. and Nabobo-Baba, U. (2014) 'Talanoa as empathic apprenticeship', *Asia Pacific Viewpoint*, 55(3): 319–330.

Frechette, J., Bitzas, V., Aubry, M., Kilpatrick, K. and Lavoie-Tremblay, M. (2020) 'Capturing lived experience: Methodological considerations for interpretive phenomenological inquiry', *International Journal of Qualitative Methods*, 19: 1–12.

Gorna, R., MacDermott, N., Rayner, C., O'Hara, M., Evans, S., Agyen, L., Nutland, W., Rogers, N. and Hastie, C. (2021) 'Long COVID guidelines need to reflect lived experience', *The Lancet*, 397(10273): 455–457.

Honey, A., Boydell, K.M., Coniglio, F., Thuy Do, T., Dunn, L., Gill, K., Glover, H., Hines, M., Scanlan, J.N. and Tooth, B. (2020) 'Lived experience research as a resource for recovery: A mixed methods study', *BMC Psychiatry*, 20(456): 1–13.

Jones, N., Atterbury, K., Byrne, L., Carras, M., Brown, M. and Phalen, P. (2021) 'Lived experience, research leadership, and the transformation of mental health services: Building a researcher pipeline', *Psychiatric Services*, 72(5): 591–593.

Lopez, L., Hart, L.H. and Katz, M.H. (2021) 'Racial and ethnic health disparities related to COVID-19', *Journal of the American Medical Association*, 325(8): 719–720.

McIntosh, I. and Wright, S. (2019) 'Exploring what the notion of "lived experience" offers for social policy analysis', *Journal of Social Policy*, 48(3): 449–467.

Petitmengin, C., Remillieux, A. and Valenzuela-Moguillansky, C. (2019) 'Discovering the structures of lived experience: Towards a micro-phenomenological analysis method', *Phenomenology and the Cognitive Sciences*, 18(4): 691–730.

Ravulo, J. (2016a) 'An integrated case management model to assist Pacific youth offenders and their families in Australia', *Care Management Journals*, 17(4): 170–179.

Ravulo, J. (2016b) 'Pacific youth offending within an Australian context', *Youth Justice*, 16(1): 34–48.

Ravulo, J. (2019) 'Raising retention rates towards achieving vocational and career aspirations in Pacific communities', *International Journal of Lifelong Education*, 38(2): 214–231.

Ravulo, J., Winterstein, U. and Said, S. (2021) *Mental Health Talanoa (MHT) Research and Resources: Collaborative Community Engagement Enhancing Mental Health and Wellbeing across Pacific Communities*, Wollongong: University of Wollongong. Available from: http://nla.gov.au/nla.obj-2949412205 [Accessed 19 December 2022].

Rogoff, B., Dahl, A. and Callanan, M. (2018) 'The importance of understanding children's lived experience', *Developmental Review*, 50(Part A): 5–15.

Tecun (Daniel Hernandez), A., Hafoka, 'Inoke, 'Ulu'ave, L. and 'Ulu'ave-Hafoka, M. (2018) 'Talanoa: Tongan epistemology and Indigenous research method', *AlterNative: An International Journal of Indigenous Peoples*, 14(2): 156–163.

Vaioleti, T. (2013) 'Talanoa: Differentiating the talanoa research methodology from phenomenology, narrative, Kaupapa Maori and feminist methodologies', *Reo, Te*, 56: 191–212.

9

The potential of lived experience-led knowledge to dismantle the academy

Caroline Lenette and Maree Higgins

Key points

- Expertise and insights based on lived experience dismantle academic norms about what constitutes knowledge and whose perspectives are valued in this context, thus contributing to epistemic justice.
- While academic research continues to privilege some forms of knowledge over others, and engagement with lived experience-led knowledge can be limited, the expertise shared in this book demonstrates the strengths of lived experience-led scholarship that no other approach to research can replicate.
- Three main characteristics of lived experience-led research that make it distinctive from other approaches are that it is unapologetically personal, inherently intersectional and undeniably visible.
- There are several tensions linked to the politics of editing contributions drawn from lived experience for an academic publication, many of which remain unresolved.

Introduction

In her book *Community as Rebellion: A Syllabus for Surviving Academia as a Woman of Color*, Professor of Latinx Studies, Lorgia García-Peña describes how academia continues to privilege specific knowledge to the detriment of other ways of knowing, a deeply entrenched 'culture' that is slow to change: 'Academia's power resides precisely in its exclusivity and exclusion. Knowledge, as imagined by the university, is measured by its proximity to particular notions of civility that are grounded ... on the Eurocentric, colonial, patriarchal, heteronormative, and white supremacist understanding of the world' (García Peña, 2022: 93). In the process of establishing and reinforcing the status quo over centuries, academic research has delegitimised forms of knowledge such as lived experience expertise, labelled as 'non-scientific', and 'dismissed [them] as unsystematic, irrational, and false' (Alonso Bejarano et al, 2019: 28). The silencing of epistemologies (or epistemic injustices), perspectives and knowledge grounded in diverse lived experiences has produced a partial understanding only of social justice issues, often lacking in intersectional nuances.

The knowledge conveyed in each chapter of this book demonstrates quality and integrity, negates the silencing and manipulation of lived experience in contemporary academia, and contributes towards epistemic justice. The authors' complex accounts situated in their everyday realities and socio-cultural contexts offer new angles on each social justice issue – not in a tentative way, but through strong assertions about what they know best. Their views are in sharp contrast with some of the outdated, formulaic and oftentimes harmful practices that social justice researchers (and academia more generally) reproduce without questioning. This approach aligns with Phipps (2019) who asks us to stop pretending that dominant forms of knowledge are the *only* way of knowing, and to instead turn to lived experience as a more authentic approach to understanding and addressing social injustices: '[E]xperts by experience, where experience is often carried through generations, have much that is stored in the scars and in the skin, and to know in these ways means taking a journey away from books and firewall-protected double-blind peer-reviewed articles in top-ranked journals' (Phipps, 2019: 6). The carefully crafted content from each group of contributors, whom we had the privilege to collaborate with and learn from, joins together in a powerful chorus that displaces outsider perspectives in a definitive way. The strengths and uniqueness of these narratives can serve to dismantle academic standards constricting what knowledge is valued. As such, lived experience-led research disrupts the norms that determine whose perspectives are recognised or ignored in the academy, and addresses epistemic injustices in scholarship by privileging the perspectives of experts by experience (Beresford et al, 2023).

The act of dismantling or pulling things apart also implies that we put forward or create new models – these are perhaps new to academic contexts but not to experts by experience. Ethical models based on lived experience-led knowledge value everyday insights and strategies and can establish new research and writing standards, which is what we have aimed to achieve in this edited collection. The key 'moral, academic and practical messages, and insights' (Mohamed et al, 2023: 1284) that only authors with lived experiences can share through their work make an important contribution to social justice research.

Potential of lived experience-led scholarship

We understand knowledge and expertise grounded in lived experience and everyday realities very differently now that we have collaborated closely with this diverse group of authors. We suspected that we would learn much from experts by experience, but we did not anticipate the depth of their impact.

Their narratives not only disrupt the academy and its knowledge production conventions, but also trouble our own understanding of person-centred and participatory research approaches. When we consider the book in its entirety, what becomes clear is that there are strengths to lived experience-led scholarship that no other approach to research can replicate.

We resist here the pressure to universalise the key points based on contributions across the three parts of the book, because it would be problematic and even unethical to summarise such complex tensions and standpoints in one or two paragraphs. For example, some authors provide insights on the development of scholarly frameworks and collaborative research models, while others' contributions are more geared towards practice and creative knowledge sharing. To reiterate Moran and colleagues' (2022) point from Chapter 1, we reject the idea of singular 'truths' and tidy narratives that must be neatly packaged for readers. Instead, we propose three main characteristics of lived experience-led research and scholarship, which demonstrate its potential to dismantle dominant epistemologies or ways of knowing in academia. We identified these characteristics through our reading of the key learnings from each chapter and considered how these can complement or challenge the practices we have encountered in social justice-focused research over several years. Lived experience-led research is unapologetically personal, inherently intersectional and undeniably visible.

Unapologetically personal

The authors' accounts dismantle the myth of objectivity as a set characteristic of 'good' academic research. Their practices, collaborations and reflections demonstrate that, to understand lived experiences of complex and multifaceted issues, we should fully engage with subjective descriptions. We should do this as a priority and a privilege, not as an afterthought or means to an end. The personal leads to deep engagement, and its dismissal to disengagement and deep pain (see Chapter 1 on the implications of being wronged as a 'knower'). This is most evident in first-hand recollections from Rebecca Moran (Chapter 3), the men under the radar (Chapter 4) and Estelle Keerthana Ramaswamy (Chapter 7) who share knowledge and expertise based on memories and reflections on significant life events that shape their understanding of and engagement in knowledge production. We also learn from personal and collaborative insights as core elements to ethical research across contexts, such as Chrysant Lily Kusumowardoyo and colleagues' descriptions of the difficulties they encountered in collaborative research with persons with disabilities in Indonesia (Chapter 5), Uncle Stan Grant (Senior) and co-authors' Indigenous-led storytelling on renewing Wiradyuri language and wisdom (Chapter 2) and Atem Dau Atem and Maree Higgins' reflections on co-research in refugee studies (Chapter 6).

Learning from subjective experiences demands a level of vulnerability, defined here as a strength and a practice that improves the quality, authenticity and the ethical nature of research (Jakimow, 2020; Lenette, 2022). By this, we mean vulnerability on the part of authors who chose to share deeply personal and at times painful insights relating to research, teaching and advocacy, and vulnerability on the part of readers to consider the book's content from a place of humility and openness to the impact the authors' expertise might have on them. As a first step, this learning experience means recognising the urge to impose (dominant) academic frames of reference to critique subjective content – a tendency we unlearned ourselves through continual engagement with authors – to truly consider and understand the key messages and knowledge each chapter conveys. In doing so, we increase recognition of lived experience as a form of knowledge or expertise in its own right towards epistemic justice.

Vulnerability can also imply feelings of distress and helplessness, sometimes resulting in uncertainty about what we can do to meaningfully address injustices that affect every aspect of people's daily realities (Lenette, 2022). We should not shy away from distress and sadness in research. As editors, we have experienced these feelings over several months, alongside the joy and pride of seeing chapters come together. From the time we read first drafts, we paid attention to the content that unsettled us. But as we state in Chapter 1, we did not want to 'sanitise' lived experience accounts to fit pre-determined models of academic scholarship or to make for a comfortable read. Our responsibility was to present contributors' subjective narratives in all their complexity and richness, including what might be distressing for readers.

We noted that the distress or sadness we felt was often due to the discrepancy between our general knowledge on the topic in focus (based on dominant narratives in the literature and social discourses), and what people with lived experiences *know* about each issue. In Chapter 4, for instance, Stephen Lake and collaborators (including anonymous contributors) describe in no uncertain terms how mental health systems fail them and the devastating impacts on their day-to-day lives. They were meticulous in their preparation of creative works that conveyed unique, personal insights, resulting in a complete shift in how we now understand suicidal ideation and mental health.

We suggest that past research initiatives might have missed opportunities to present findings that are considered too personal and 'messy' to be included in academic publications, when these were in fact the *main* concerns. At best, using quotes as snippets of lived experiences to 'illustrate' so-called expert scholars' points of view to legitimise outsider-imposed gazes is purely utilitarian or a tokenistic form of engagement (Lenette, 2022). When we *free* lived experience from the constraints of academic priorities based on colonial values, we enter a relational space that is decidedly unpredictable and discomforting. It then becomes impossible to support utilitarian models given the unique insights that lived experience-led scholarship brings. There have been many calls to embrace messiness in research rather than attempt to 'tidy up' key learnings because of the rich knowledge that can be overlooked (for example, Law, 2004; Cook, 2009; Lenette, 2020; 2022). This is a principle we would like to see integrated more systematically in future social justice-focused research.

Inherently intersectional

The authors' expertise and stories dismantle the myth of universal experiences as a decolonial strategy. Our observation of research practices in recent decades is that so much of the social justice literature is still unilateral. Academia's obsession with categorising experiences according to disciplinary silos means that we can easily miss the intersections and nuances of complex everyday realities. A major issue with these artificial research structures is that they can deny intersectional concerns that affect people the most. In contrast, a focus on lived experience is, by definition, intersectional (see Chapter 1) because subjective standpoints are grounded in unique realities and identities, shaped by socio-cultural knowledge. Even when we consider the impacts of collective experiences such as the COVID-19 pandemic, there are specificities and contextual factors that demand tailored and culturally safe strategies, as Jioji Ravulo and colleagues highlight in Chapter 8. In this example, the danger of using vague categorisations such as 'culturally and linguistically diverse' rather than recognising, centring and valuing Pasifika wisdom, would result in overlooking the strengths of a *talanoa* process.

We were firmly committed to privileging intersectional perspectives in this book, and we thought carefully about potential contributors. As a result, we struggled to find the right authors for Chapter 5. We had worked with disability studies scholars for some time, but noted that all were white, middle-class and English speaking. Fortunately for us, Chrysant Lily Kusumowardoyo and Husna Yuni Wulansari published a journal article in 2022 (see Further reading, Chapter 1), which analysed the intersectional nature of lived experiences of disability in Indonesia. We invited these researchers, and eventually their co-authors, precisely because they were not based in a western country or academic institution, as we aimed to prioritise new perspectives. We had a similar experience with developing our collaboration with Estelle Keerthana Ramaswamy (Chapter 7). We wanted to challenge the lack of majority-world perspectives on trans and gender diverse lived experience – a gap highlighted in her chapter – because such intersectional considerations would define unique expressions of gender identities and highlight injustices from a different angle. The literature we were familiar with did not reflect those considerations until we came across Estelle's work on social media.

To bring intersectionality to the fore, we asked all authors to include positionality statements in their reflections, so that we (and readers) would understand the intersectional standpoints that informed the chapter. We wanted to illustrate that high quality research should be intersectional – otherwise, we are just rehashing narrow views devoid of nuances that characterise reality. Since stating positionalities is a core practice in our teaching and research, we *assumed* that this was a shared norm. However, we had to reassess this assumption when our collaborators from Indonesia asked us what we meant by positionality. We considered that we had perhaps imposed a western-centric notion across vastly different contexts. However, the dialogue that ensued with these authors led to new understandings on the purpose of being reflexive about positionalities and the usefulness of explicitly stating this in academic writing.

For Estelle Keerthana Ramaswamy, defining and stating her positionality was central to establishing the intersectional lens that informed Chapter 7, especially in a polemic, trans-exclusionary context where the very existence of trans people is contested, and where research models can be culturally unsafe. Chapter 2, which Wiradyuri Elder Uncle Stan Grant (Senior) led, shows how integral positionality is to Indigenous research, practices and writing – not as an afterthought but very much at the centre of decolonising knowledge production.

Thus, the inherently intersectional and nuanced nature of lived experience is better reflected in scholarship based on unique first-hand accounts. To echo our discussion in Chapter 1, one lived experience does not represent all experiences of similar issues. We anticipate that, as researchers and experts by experience collaboratively create more pathways for lived experience-led narratives in academia, we will engage with a multitude of stories and views that remain marginalised. Drawing on the strengths of intersectional approaches can lead to deeper understandings of social justice issues.

Undeniably visible

The authors' diverse knowledges dismantle academic structures that intentionally make some lived experiences invisible despite claiming to promote participation and 'inclusion'. As we recalled in the Preface, we were pleased that all invited contributors were immediately positive about the book's focus, given the limited opportunities to publish such scholarship elsewhere. Initially, some authors did not think they had anything interesting to say in the context of an academic publication – something we had to work on together! We consciously developed a safe and supportive writing space for contributors to explore how they could make the intimate knowledge on their day-to-day experiences visible to readers. In addition to finding the writing and editing process validating, the authors were quickly able to draw on a range of invigorating as well as painful perspectives to unpack and articulate key learnings based on their lived experiences. For us, this enthusiasm re-emphasised the general lack of meaningful opportunities for people with first-hand experiences to contribute to academic discourses on social justice issues (see also Beresford et al, 2023).

One example is Stephen Lake and colleagues (Chapter 4) for whom reflecting on their positionalities was a new task that other research processes had not supported. By thinking about their positionalities, they found connection and relief, the joy of recognising and being recognised by others. Documenting such personal information was poignant, prompting reflexivity among the men about the impact of becoming visible, and, for some of the authors, resulting in the choice to remain under the radar through anonymous authorship.

Even though visibility of perspectives in academia is determined by the norms of the colonial project (as García Peña's earlier quote reminds us), the chapter authors rejected this structure and came up with their own writing frameworks and disruptive methodologies of knowledge production. There was no interest to reproduce abstract or obscure content. Their approach to writing means that the content is more accessible and relatable. As we state in Chapter 1, Alonso Bejarano and colleagues (2019: 28) argue that changing writing styles in academia is closely linked to challenging what counts as valid knowledge, in that '[a] limited perspective on what counts as research leads to similarly limited forms of writing – academic essays and books, laden with jargon, perpetually citing the same authorities, speaking to a restricted audience of experts'. We can no longer afford to rely solely on such sources, which often sabotage efforts to effect change. Instead, we should collaboratively create more research and writing opportunities where lived experience-led scholarship leads the way. We do not suggest completely disregarding the abundant existing literature on social justice topics, but we do argue that, without firm commitments to shifting the balance towards lived experience-led discourses, this area of research will not progress in meaningful ways.

Reflections

Caroline

What I enjoyed the most about editing this book was coming across 'unexpected' stories. Each chapter surprised me in a unique way. Each perspective taught me a lot. I felt engaged in a process where writers 'reversed the gaze'. I felt privy to so many rich insights that I had never considered before, with a lot of 'ah ha!' moments. I experienced a range of emotions, from pride and hope to sadness and anger. Sometimes, I had to set drafts aside to reflect on the candid stories the authors had generously shared. I was touched by their trust in the process, especially when we had never met some of them (including anonymous authors). Their initial reaction in response to the book idea motivated me to keep thinking about ways to honour their narratives and expertise in the context of an academic publication. I very much enjoyed witnessing how some authors, who were initially timid about expressing their views, exercised agency when deciding how their chapter should be finalised. This was precisely the purpose of creating this publication space.

What I found the most difficult was to resist imposing a writing style or academic frame of reference on the work of first-time authors. As an experienced writer, I was conscious that supporting new authors to express their perspectives in a book chapter format would present specific challenges. Our aim was to offer enough constructive feedback for the next iteration of the draft without over-editing their work or using a pre-determined lens to evaluate their contributions. For each chapter, I asked myself: How do I maintain the authenticity of their contributions? Will it make sense to readers if the author/s use/s this word or this expression? Mohamed and colleagues (2023) encountered similar tensions while editing academic papers for a special issue of the *British Journal of Social Work* on 'Voice and Influence of People with Lived Experience'.

At times, we provided feedback based on what we anticipated the reviewers might find unclear – I'm still not sure whether this was justified. Based on several years of reading, interpreting and responding to positive and not so constructive reviewer feedback, especially for peer-reviewed journal articles, we were conscious of our 'in-between' role. We found ourselves wondering how we could act as 'buffers' between the review process and the excitement and vulnerability that authors expressed about their chapters. But we also acknowledged that we cannot anticipate how readers will receive the material, as this is beyond our control. At the same time, we did not want to be patronising; many of these authors have no doubt dealt with difficult receptions, responses and feedback when sharing their views in different contexts.

We were especially mindful of how the content might affect readers with the same identity or with similar lived experiences, especially when the stories were distressing. Because of these considerations, it was crucial to clearly communicate the rationale for some of the suggested changes to authors with ample opportunity to discuss alternatives. I know how daunting it can be to receive feedback on work that centres subjective experiences: suggestions for editing can hurt more. Ultimately, I felt that we had good relationships with each group of authors, and we could ask for and respect their wishes as well as suggest how to improve the text and achieve the aims of the book.

Maree

What I enjoyed the most about editing this book were the encounters with people who care deeply about social justice and lived experience, as I do. Where authors experienced uncertainty during the writing process, one question would ground their narrative time and time again: who do you imagine reading this chapter and what do you imagine is their reaction? The question of *who* we are writing for and *why* we are documenting these narratives is, I think, fundamental to social justice research. In this project, I found people's answers to these questions, in every case, both clarifying and uplifting. How we each responded to these central questions is the thrum that pulses through this book, the generator at the heart of this exploration of lived experience-led scholarship.

What I found the most difficult was to preserve space in my work role for this uplifting and unique collaborative experience. I have often heard that the deep commitment of time, energy and self in lived experience research is very poorly acknowledged and valued by universities. I have certainly witnessed this while writing and co-editing this book. I have also observed how so many of my colleagues – passionate, justice-oriented and dedicated – tie themselves into knots in order to respond professionally and consistently to the multitude of demands placed upon us in the hungry and lean work environment that is the modern university. When speaking with a trusted manager about the serious injury I had at the beginning of 2022, I was encouraged to 'ease up on my research' for a period, rather than being relieved of any of the responsibilities I was carrying. Constant learning, self-questioning, critical reflection and mutual care were hallmarks of this project; yet I often felt like I had to hide the enormity of this commitment behind a shield of efficiency and agreeability. This exacted a weighty toll on myself and those closest to me.

The genuine commitment of authors to the goals of this project was particularly heartening and humbling in this stressful context. We were heartened to see authors' willingness to name problems with their organisations and to describe challenges they experienced with lived experience-led research. For example, a senior academic initiated Chapter 4 on the 'Under the Radar' men's suicide prevention project, and the initial draft included perspectives from paid staff. However, after much discussion, the senior academic and the group decided to prioritise the men's perspectives to produce a frank and fearless project critique. The men's narratives took centre stage, with the continued support of staff who were involved in the research.

Another example of commitment to these goals was the willingness of the lead authors of Chapter 5, 'Co-researching with persons with disabilities: reflections and lessons learned', to subject their research to scrutiny. While critically evaluating their research assumptions, practices and outcomes produced meaningful lessons for the future, it also potentially placed the lead researchers in precarious positions within their organisations. Their honest appraisal of what they didn't do well could invite unjustified scrutiny and reduce institutional trust in the team's capabilities. Such findings can ripple through structures of power in unforeseen ways.

This highlights another aspect that we were especially mindful of while editing this book – the uncertainty continuum. Caroline Lenette has described some of the uncertainties we experienced while editing chapter drafts. We also faced uncertainty because of our respect and care for how authors might share community knowledge because we know that so many research practices are still extractive and reflect outsider gazes. Further, our discussions with Estelle Keerthana Ramaswamy about requests for changes led to reflections on how those suggestions seemed to reinforce rather than combat the 'colonially pathologised universalisation' they discuss in their chapter. Another example of uncertainty related to our collaboration with two highly respected colleagues from African countries who were thrilled to find a home for a piece of writing they had been working on for some time. However, because of complex visa-related issues, it became impossible for them to prioritise this task. The lead author had to withdraw their chapter so that both could focus on what was most important to them – obtaining safe passage to their destinations.

Conclusion

As Alonso Bejarano and colleagues (2019: 38–39) state: '[t]he suggestion that the way they do research needs to be rethought will likely make many people angry and uncomfortable. But for a new generation of scholars discontented with the demands and restrictions that the colonial model imposes, such a call may feel liberating'. Perhaps this edited collection will prompt others (within and outside the academy) to add their own contributions to lived experience-led scholarship. We see this book as a starting point for more collaborative work and writing, and hopefully as a model that others want to draw on and replicate (see also Beresford et al, 2023 in their special issue of the *British Journal of Social Work* on lived experience). While we firmly believe in the potential of lived experience-led knowledge and scholarship to disrupt and decolonise the academy, we remain conscious of the ongoing challenges to dismantle entrenched norms in research and knowledge production. We know that there are multiple obstacles to changing a long-standing system of knowledge production and that significant changes towards epistemic justice rarely occur overnight. However, we are confident that, with the dedication and commitment of experts by experience such as the ones we had the privilege to work with, change will eventuate.

Further reading

Bezzina, L. (2018) 'The role of indigenous and external knowledge in development interventions with disabled people in Burkina Faso: The implications of engaging with lived experiences', *Disability and the Global South*, 5(2): 1488–1507.

Grundman, S.H., Edri, N. and Stanger Elran, R. (2021) 'From lived experience to experiential knowledge: A working model', *Mental Health and Social Inclusion*, 25(1): 23–31.

Kia, H., MacKinnon, K.R. and Göncü, K. (2022) 'Harnessing the lived experience of transgender and gender diverse people as practice knowledge in social work: A standpoint analysis', *Affilia*, 38(2): 190–205.

Voronka, J. (2016) 'The politics of "people with lived experience": Experiential authority and the risks of strategic essentialism', *Philosophy, Psychiatry, & Psychology*, 2(3): 189–201.

References

Alonso Bejarano, C., López Juárez, L., Mijangos García, M.A. and Goldstein, D.M. (2019) *Decolonizing Ethnography: Undocumented Immigrants and New Directions in Social Science*, Durham, NC: Duke University Press.

Beresford, P., Golding, F., Hughes, M., Levin, L., Mohamed, O., Schön, U.-K. and Unwin, P. (2023) 'Editorial – special issue', *The British Journal of Social Work*, 53(3): 1275–1281.

Cook, T. (2009) 'The purpose of mess in action research: Building rigour though a messy turn', *Educational Action Research*, 17(2): 277–291.

García Peña, L. (2022) *Community as Rebellion: A Syllabus for Surviving Academia as a Woman of Color*, Chicago: Haymarket Books.

Jakimow, T. (2020) 'Risking the self: Vulnerability and its uses in research', in P. Wadds, N. Apoifis, S. Schmeidl and K. Spurway (eds) *Navigating Fieldwork in the Social Sciences: Stories of Danger, Risk and Reward*, London: Palgrave Macmillan, pp 147–161.

Law, J. (2004) *After Method: Mess is Social Science Research*, Oxfordshire: Routledge.

Lenette, C. (2020) 'Sitting with the mess', in P. Wadds, N. Apoifis, S. Schmeidl and K. Spurway (eds) *Navigating Fieldwork in the Social Sciences: Stories of Danger, Risk and Reward*, London: Palgrave Macmillan, pp 39–60.

Lenette, C. (2022) *Participatory Action Research: Ethics and Decolonization*, New York: Springer.

Mohamed, O., Schön, U.K. and Unwin, P. (2023) 'Introduction to academic papers section', *The British Journal of Social Work*, 53(3): 1282–1284.

Moran, R.J., Martin, R. and Ridley, S. (2022) ' "It helped me open my eyes": Incorporating lived experience perspectives in social work education', *Affilia*, (88610992211073): 1–16.

Phipps, A. (2019) *Decolonising Multilingualism: Struggles to Decreate*, Bristol: Multilingual Matters.

Index

www.ingramcontent.com/pod-product-compliance
Lightning Source LLC
Chambersburg PA
CBHW070625030426
42337CB00020B/3919